A HISTORY (

By Anne Andrews

1. TIXALL'S CHURCHES

A history of a small village church and some of its connections.

ISBN 0 9527425 1 9

Published 1995 by Hanyards Press
c/o 2, The Hanyards, Tixall, Stafford ST18 0XY
Printed by Counterprint, Tipping St, Stafford

INTRODUCTION

This is intended to be the first book in a series covering various aspects of the History of Tixall.

It is hoped that future booklets will cover topics such as:- Tixall People; Tixall Burials; Tixall Hall; Tixall Village; Tixall Farms and Agriculture; Tixall Industries,eg. Quarries and Brickworks.

Information has been derived from a variety of sources including the Shrewsbury and other papers in the Staffordshire County Record Office; the Plea Rolls and other papers published by the Staffordshire Historic Society; various documents at the William Salt Library, Stafford; and a variety of other published sources. A full list of references is given at the end.

Thanks are expressed to the County Record Office, William Salt Library, Lichfield Joint Record Office, Lichfield Diocesan Registry, Godfrey Bostock, National Railway Museum, Landmark Trust, Staffordshire Newsletter, and everyone else who has provided help and support.

This book is dedicated to all those who worship or have worshipped at Tixall Church.

All profits from the sale of this book will go towards Tixall Church, which is currently facing extensive roof repairs.

CONTENTS

Introduction.

1. EARLY HISTORY

Christianity was established in the area when St Chad, Bishop of the Mercians, established his see at Lichfield in 669 - 672 [1]

There is no record of a church at Tixall in the Domesday Survey of 1086, despite the presence of two Manors worth 30/- and 10/- respectively.

Domesday refers to three previous Saxon land-holders:- Almund in the smaller manor, possibly based on Hanyards, and Alric and Ordmer in the larger manor possibly based on Brancote and Tixall Village. Alric and Ordmer were free men.[2] According to Clifford,[3] Alric appears to have been a royal thane, the highest rank of nobility and held various other estates including part of Ridware.

With this evidence of a significant number of people living in the area it seems quite likely that they would have been a small Saxon Church at Tixall, probably made of timber.

Gerard FitzBrian, a wealthy burgess of Stafford provided 70 acres of meadowland called Sheepwash Meadow, the portion of the River Sow adjoining it, and some property in Stafford subject to a yearly rent of 8s for the Augustinian Canons from Darley Abbey in Derbyshire to establish a new priory near Stafford in 1174.[4,5]

Richard Peche, Bishop of Lichfield, and a close friend of Thomas A'Beckett who was murdered in 1170, completed the building of the Priory at St Thomas's in 1180. At the Dissolution in the 1530s it was the 4th richest religious house in Staffordshire after Burton, Tutbury and Dieula Cross, being valued at £141 - 13s - 2d in October 1538.

However, Tixall was never under the control of St Thomas's, having been a free chapel under the jurisdiction of the Dean of the

Collegiate Church of St Mary, Stafford, alongwith the parishes of Ingestre, Castlechurch, Cresswell, St Nicholas's Chapel at Stafford Castle, and the hospitals of St John and St Leonard in Forebridge.[1]

Because St Mary's was too far from Tixall for the inhabitants to walk there regularly for services, the Lord of the Manor of Tixall probably presented a petition to the Dean or College of St Mary's, for leave to erect a chapel for the performance of Divine Service by a priest paid for and maintained by the Lord of the Manor, in return for which St Mary's would receive all the offerings.[4]

This was probably granted on condition that burials, marriages, etc. took place at St Mary's,and that the inhabitants of Tixall attended St Mary's on Easter Day and other Festivals. The Lord of the Manor would have later endowed the Church in the usual way. As this would relieve the Dean of St Mary's of all responsibility, he would then allow the Lord of the Manor to present clerks to perform Divine Service and receive all offerings, merely reserving to himself the pension of 6s 8d.

Peganus de Gastenois, ancestor of the De Wasteneys, was Lord of the Manor of Tixall from 1176 to 1193, having inherited them from his father Geoffrey.[5]

The right of presenting the priest, or holding the advowson for a church, had financial benefit for the holder, and was therefore frequently the subject of litigation.

In a lengthy court case in 1247 - 1250[7,8,9] the King, Henry III, sued another Pagan de Wasteneys for the advowson of the church of Tikeshale, and the jury found that the ancestors of Pagan had presented to a vacancy when in England, and when abroad, the Dean of the King's Chapel of St Mary, Stafford, had presented until Geoffrey de Wasteneys in the reign of King John [1199 - 1216] had deprived the chapel of the right of presentation.

It is suggested that another Payne de Wasteneys was murdered by Stephen while staying in William the chaplains house c1199, and his body, which had been buried there, was removed by his son Geoffrey some 50 years later.[5] " and that the said chapel always had the liberty until one Geoffrey de Wasteneys, the ancestor of the said Pagan, in the reign of King John, carried away a certain corpse which ought to have been buried there, and caused it to be buried at *(left blank)* , and afterwards presented his Clerk to the Bishop against the liberty aforesaid"[6] - thereby infringing the rights of the Dean & Chapter of St Mary's Stafford, who claimed the free chapel of Tixall.

This shows that there was a chapel at Tixall c1199, possibly with a chaplain called William, and the chapel had probably been there for some time.

Around 1250, John Meveral - Rector of the Church of Ticksall, is a witness for some deeds at Kniveton near Ashbourne,[10] but in this case Ticksall may have been confused with Ticknall, near Ashby de la Zouche.

In 1288 another dispute arose between Eva de Oswaldestre, who had inherited custody of the heir of Henry de Wasteney, another Geoffrey who was under age, and his lands, including the advowson of the Chapel of Tixhale, through her husband, Adam de Chetwynde[11] - "As Geoffrey could not controvert these facts, a verdict is given for Eva."

In 1286 Geoffrey de Wasteneys, Parson of the Church of Tykeshale was fined 40s for transgressions in Cannock Forest.[12]

Sons of the Lord of the Manor were often made 'Clerks' and instituted to a benefice at any age. The Bishop then had power over the youth to place him under a tutor and sequestrate the income of the benefice to his education. This was used as a method of educating younger sons.[13]

In 1296 King Edward I seized all the lay fees, goods and chattels of the clergy.[14] A long list of these was drawn up in February 1297, so that they could be restored when a subsidy of 1/5 had been paid. This gives Richard de Bisshopeston as the parson of Tixall.

In 1324, John Maynard, citizen and mercer of London, and Henry Polsted, armiger, were the complainants against Henry Stafford, Lord Stafford and Ursula his wife, deforciants of various properties, tithes and church pensions including: "..the tithes of all grain, sheaves, corn, hay, fruits, wool, lambs, fowls, calves, young pigs, geese, eggs, milk, cheese, flax & hemp, annually renewing, growing, arising and happening in" various places including "Tyxsall Parisshe"; "and of a pension of 6s 8d by the year issueing from the rectory and church of Tyxsall, and of 3s 4d every three years for the procurations issueing from the rectory and church of Tyxsall".[15] A Similar cases were brought in 1435,[16] 1458,[17] 1563,[18] 1564,[19] and 1610,[20] when the tithes and pension were still 6s 8d with the three yearly procurations of 3s 4d.

In 1326 Geoffrey de Wasteneys is again re-establishing his right to the Manor of Tyxsale and the Advowson of the Church, which he had given to Roger de Aston, Parson of the Church of Weston.[21]

There were strong links between the Manor of Hanyards and the Early Chapel at Ingestre, which was nearer to the Hanyards than the present church at Ingestre.
In 1305, Hugh de Hanenyate acknowledged the manor of Haveneyate to be the right of Roger Toly, Chaplain of Ingestre.[22]
In 1323 Ralph de Haveneyate ie. Hanyards, Chaplain , is suing Richard de Coppenhale and Isabella his wife for land at Hopton.[23]
Further court cases occur in 1479 and 1481, when Thomas Counter, Chaplain of Ingestre is occupying 1/3 part of the manor of Hanyat.[24]

In the time of Henry VII (1485 - 1509) William Chetwynd built a chapel to St Erasmus, Bishop and Martyr in Diocletian's day 284 - 304, on the "waste of Ingestre". It subsequently became famous for certain springs of salt and medicinal waters adjoining it, and was frequented by lame and diseased persons.[4]

The Tax List or Subsidy Roll of 1327[25] for Tixall, includes "Henrico Atte chirchende" (or Henry at the Church end of the village ?) with the 3rd highest payment after Geoffrey de Wasteneys and Johanna de Beumus. Similarly the Roll for 1332 - 1333 includes Malcolm de Wasteneys, John son of William, and then "Isolda atte chirche Yerd.[26]

In 1339 King Edward III sued Malcolm de Wasteneys and his son John, for the next presentation to the King's free chapel of Tyckesale.[27] In 1402 Roger Wasteneys was being granted the advowson of the free chapel of Tyxhale.[28]

In 1366 Roger de Sulgrave is described as Clerk residing at Tixhale and possessing the free chapel of Tixhale, sinecure(*ie. a benefice without cure of souls, or which has no work or duties attached to it)*; taxed at 10 marks.[29]

The last of the line of Tixall De Wasteneys was Rose, who married Sir John Merston, and sold the Manor of Tixall to Sir Thomas Littleton, the judge, in 1469.

The Manor remained in the Littleton Family, passing to the Astons in 1507, when Joan Littleton married Sir John Aston of Haywood.

There appears to be no record of the names of any Rectors for Tixall Church for this period from William de Hanlegh in 1387 to Robert Lokke in 1533.

RECTORS OR PRIESTS OF TIXALL

Year	Name	Years	Description
c1250	John Meverel ?	?	Rector[10]
1286	Geoffrey de Wasteney	10?	Parson[12,4]
1296	Richard de Bisshopeston	70?	Parson[14,4]
1366	Roger de Sulgrave	21?	Clerk[29,4]
1387	William de Hanlegh	?	Rector[4]
?	?		
1533	Robert Lokke	15?	Rector[4]
1548	Samson Burne	9	Rector[4,32]
1557	Thomas Sherrade	29	Rector/Chaplain[4,32]
1586	Ralph Smith	46	Rector[4,32]
1632	Robert Jones M.A.	7	Rector[4,32]
1639	Jeremy Morral B.A.	6	Rector[4,32]
1645	Thomas Harward B.A.	3	Rector[4,32]
1648	Daniel Bayley	28	Rector[4,32]
1676	Ralph Phillips	4	Rector[4,32,36]
1680	Simon Wakelyn	18	Rector[4]
1698	Richard/Mathew Drakeford	9	Rector[4]
1707	Thomas Holbroke	12	Rector[4]
1719	Thomas Loxdale	23	Rector[4,51]
1732	John Robinson		Curate
1742	Ralph Turner	19	Rector[4,55,56]
1761	William Corne	60	Rector[4]
1823	Thomas Walker	8?	Rector[73]

1823 -1831	Succession of Curates	12[4]	
1813	John Clarke		Curate
1823	Ed.J.Rathbone		Curate
1824	J.W.Tomlinson		Curate
1826	Joseph Smith		Curate[74]

RECTORS OR PRIESTS OF TIXALL (CONT.)

Year	Name	Years	Description
1831	William Webb	52	Rector[4]
1884	Craven Jervis Vincent	22	Rector
1906	James W.Walton	5	Rector[4]
1910	Harold Smith	21	Rector[4]
1931	Hon.Sydney G.W.Maitland	7	Rector*[4]
1938	Clifford William Dugmore	5	Rector*[4]
1943	W.F.O'Neill Fisher	10	Rector*
1953	A.Hanley.Towlson	4	Rector*
1958	P.H.Vaughan	5	Rector*
1965	Arthur Poole	14	Rector*
1981	E.G.H.Townshend	6	Rector**
1988	John Gear	4	Rector**
1993	Roger Vaughan		Rector**

* Joint Benefice with Ingestre
** Joint Benefice with Ingestre and Littleworth

2. POST 1500: EARLY CATHOLICS & PROTESTANTS

A list giving the value of livings, etc. within the Deanery of Stafford in 1536 shows Tixall Church valued at £8 - 7s - 4d, compared with Ingestre at £10 -16s - 8d, with Spiritualties or a pension of 6s - 8d compared with 3s - 4d for Ingestre.[4]

The greater value of Ingestre was due to the increased alms from the adjacent healing springs.

In the early 1500's the English Church was still under the Pope in Rome with mass being celebrated in Latin. In 1533 King Henry VIII broke with Rome, and by the Act of Supremacy in 1534 appointed himself "Supreme Head of the Church of England". An English Bible was to be provided in every Church, and Parish Registers of Baptisms, Marriages and Burials kept in a Parish Chest or a "sure coffer".

The Royal Free chapels, including St Mary's Stafford, were dissolved in 1548 under an Act of 1847[1]. From this date Tixall and Ingestre would have been separate Parish Churches and responsible for their own burials.

Then in 1549 under Edward VI, the Act of Uniformity introduced a new, simple form of worship with the Holy Communion celebrated in English for the first time, and Church Plate being confiscated by the Crown. Images were destroyed and church walls whitewashed.

Cranmer produced the first Book of Common Prayer in English in 1549, and the following year, 1550, it was ordered that all Latin service books should be destroyed.[30]

When the Catholic Queen Mary Tudor came to the throne in 1553, all these changes were reversed.

An inventory of Church Goods and Ornaments taken in 1552/3,[31] shows that Tixall had:-

"Fryste two vestements, on cope,
ii surpleses
iii alter clothes
itm on towell
iii napkins
ii belles,*(In the tower or similar)* a sanctus bell;
itm on crosse of brass & a cloth for the same
ij cruetts *(small bottles for water or wine)*
itm ij corporases *(ancient eucharistic vestments or linen*
    cloths upon which the concecrated elements are
    placed, and with which they are subsequently
    covered) with on case & a little pillow"

Samson Burne, Rector of Tixall until he resigned in 1557, was one of 7 Staffordshire Incumbents who resigned during the reign of the catholic Queen Mary (1553 - 1558).[32]

He may not have approved of the strict Marian regime and persecutions, or may have been a married priest.

His successor, Thomas Sherrade, is described as Chaplain when he was instituted in 1557/8. This coincides with the building of the Elizabethan Hall at Tixall in 1555 by Sir Edward Aston.

In 1558, when Elizabeth I ascended the throne, all the changes of Queen Mary were reversed by the Elizabethan Settlement, and the Act of Uniformity in 1559.

At this time church attendance was still compulsory, with fines of 1/- a month for not attending; men and women sat separately; and there were long sermons.

The Lords of the Manor of Tixall had always been protestants, and in fact the first Sir Walter Aston, 1529 - 1589, who built the Gatehouse c1580, had been an active anti-catholic having conformed to the new religion in the time of Edward VI and Queen Elizabeth.

In 1570 Elizabeth I was excommunicated by the Pope, and the remaining Catholics became recusants because they refused to attend the services of the Church of England.

In 1579 when Father Sutton, who had been sent to Stafford Gaol with several of the local Catholic gentry, came before the court, Sir Walter Aston was the examining JP.

Sir Walter got so angry while cross-examining him, that he added point to his questions by twice striking the prisoner with his staff and knocked him down.

Sir Walter then insisted on giving evidence against him at the assizes were Sutton was duly convicted and sentenced to hanging.[33]

In April 1585 an order was given for the confiscation of recusant's armour.

The commissioners were to visit the houses of recusants without warning and demand their armour and weapons, making an indenture of what they confiscated, and informing the owners that it would be returned when they conformed.

Sufficient weapons were to be left for the owners to defend themselves.[34]

In May 1585 John Giffard, a recusant from Chillington Hall, was writing to Richard Bagot:-

" Sir, the armore which was taken from mi house to Tixall dothe take greate harme and is almost spoiled for lacke of dressing and if it would please you to wryte to Mr Philippes or to declare so muche to his servant, in casse I woldebi him make sute the same might be solde, reserving so moche to be kepte there still as I shall be charged withall to furnish either for horsemen or footemen and then that the same mae be dressed at mi charge..." [34]

Religious persecution continued, and in 1595 Agnes Plant, wife of Robert Plant of Stafford was testifying in court against John Margeryson, late of Tixall:

"nowe indicted as a ·recusant did utter these words follinge about a month last past to her this examinant viz. That he had read in a booke that the Childe should be famyshed att the mothers breast and the groundes should be destroyed with worms before Michilimas next." [35]

The first draft had been struck through and then rewritten. John appears to have been predicting the end of the world because of the religious changes and persecution.

Ralph Smith the Rector in 1586 is described as no preacher, no degree and of loose life! He had been ordained on March 21st 1584/5 by William Overton. [32]

Sir Walter Aston K.B. and Baronet First Lord Aston[3]

Sir Walter Aston's grandson, Sir Walter, 1st Lord Aston was converted to Roman Catholicism during his second visit to Spain as Ambassador from 1635 to 1638. He wrote to a friend explaining his conversion. [36] (See page 15 - 17)

In a letter dated March 7th 1638 to the Earl of Portland[37] (his son's father-in-law) explaining the will he had made when he first went to Spain, he says " I have likewise given my servant Jerome Morrell and in his wife in my life time, all such linen and goods, whatsoever in my howse, and ye Mulberrie Garden, *(His London House supposedly on the site of Buckingham Palace)* excepting ye bed and hangings in ye chamber wher I lie;......"

Presumably this is the same Jeremy Morrel who is listed as Rector of Tixall in 1639. [32]

MY DEARE FREND,

Whereas there hath been much friendship and kindness betwixt us for so long a time, I hope it shall not break of upon this occasion of my changing my religion.

Howsoever, I am, I thank God, so resolved that I had rather loose the best wordly friends that ever I had then change again from what I am.

Now, because I esteeme somewhat more of you then of an ordinary friend, I have thought good to say a little more to you of this matter then I would to everyone.

First, then, I would have you to think that I did not rashly make this change, nor upon a suddaine, but upon the best consideration and judgement that my wit could reach unto.

And although I was first very fearful and loath to forsake that religion in which I was brought up, and had lived so long, yet, when I found so many reasons for it, I resolved, without any further delayes, to betake myself to that faith and beleif wherein I am now determined to live and dye.

And if you desire to know some of these reasons which did so prevail with me, in brief I will tell you.

First, then, I had read in holy scripture of a church that was begunne by Christ and his apostles, which was built upon a rock; *(Matt.xvi)* and so strong that the gates of hell should not prevaile against it.

Againe, that the Holy Ghost was promised *(Jo.xiv)* unto his church to teache and guide her in all truthe *(Jo.xvi)*: and that this church was therefore called the pillar *(I Tim iii)*and foundation of truthe.

Againe, that those who would not heare this church were to be accompted as heathens and publicans.*(Matt xviii)*

I found also in the same holy scripture, that in this church, Christ had left a continuall succession of pastours and doctours; *(Ephes iv)* which succession should last to the world's end, that those that would be saved might not be carryed away with every blast of vaine doctrine, but remaine stedfast in truthe.

I remembered, also,that the scripture said there should be heresies *(Cor xi)*; to the end that those that were approved might be made manifest by resisting, condemning, and overthrowing those heresies.

These, and many other things, I remembred to be in holy scripture, which did no way agree to that religion whereof I was.

Then calling to minde that which I had often heard, to witt, that Martin Luther and his followers were the first beginners of that religion, I knew that many denyed it; but mee thought it was plaine enough, because no (Cont.)

books or histories did ever make mention of such a religion till now, since Luther's time, which was but little more than a hundred yeeres agoe:

Yea, I remembred, that in our owne cronicles (that speak of the most memorable things that have been done in this realme since Christ's time till now) there is mention of many religions that have been heere professed; but no mention at all of such a religion as that which the Protestants now professe.

Therefore, I thought surely, that either the true religion was never in England, or els that the Protestant's could not be it.

After this, I considered the former places of scripture, examining to what religion they did most fitly agree. Three things out of the foresaid places of scripture are cleere:

The first, that the church which Christ and his apostles founded must continue from Christ till the world's end.

The second, that in that church there is a continual succession of doctours and teachers.

Thirdly, that those heresies which have risen since Christ's time, have been still condemned by the church.

None of these three things appertains to the protestants: Therefore they are not the church of Christ.

The first appertaines not to them, because they have had no being in the world till now of late. If any man say otherwise, lett him shew in what cuntry, or kingdome, or city, or place, there was ever such a religion professed, with such a book of common prayer in English, or any other vulgar language: such a manner of doctrine about points of faith and sacraments as they hould. This they can never doe.

The second, also, concerning a continuall succession of doctours and teachers, is as impossible for them to show as the former. For they cannot show where any persons of their profession ever were; much lesse can they shew doctours and teachers of such a profession.

Lastly, the third thing about condemning and overthrowing of heresies, it is plaine that they never gathered any generall counsells to condemne them, nor used any meanes by which such heresies have been overthrowne.

Now, when I saw that these things that are in a manner marks of the true church of Christ, did not agree to the protestants, amongst whome I yet remained, I thought what other religion it might be to which they might or did agree unto: and I could finde none but the catholique Roman religion to be it. In that, although I had not much learning, I could easily perceive a being from age to age, and that many cuntries and kingdomes have continued in the same for many hundreds of yeares together.

Yea, it was plaine to me, out of our own cronicles of England, that no other religion flourished heere in this realme for almost a thousand yeares together but that.

It was plaine, also, that when we English first received this religion, we had it from Rome by St Augustine, that was a monk, and sent hither by St Gregory, that was then Pope of Rome.

This, then, was cleare concerning the first of the thre foresaid points, to witt, that this catholique Roman religion came down from Christ and his apostles, and remayned in being for all that time; which I could find in no other church but that.

And as for the second point, which was about a continuall succession of doctours and teachers, it was plaine to me also, that in that church there was such a succession. Our owne cronicles make mention of a succession of Bishops of Canterbery, all Roman catholiques, one after another, for nine hundred yeares altogether, which was from the time of Pope Gregory till the time of Edward VI in whose daies Cranmer, then Bishop of Canterbery, shewed himself a heretick, and was afterwards burned for the same.

Besides, I mett with many books wherein I saw a continuall succession of the Popes of Rome from St Peter till the present times.

Likewise I saw that the Roman catholiques could name many learned men and writers in all ages that defended and taught that religion.

Lastly, it was made cleare unto me that those heresies that did arise from time to time in the world, they did still bend most of their forces against that catholique Roman church; and she it was that gathered general counsells against those heresies to condemne their false doctrines, and by her, in processe of time, they were overthrowne.

Much more I could say out of those good books, which, since I left being a protestant, I have read. But this shal be sufficient to lett you know what reason I had to become a catholique. And I thank God I finde now by experience many other reasons to confirme me more and more therein.

ASTON

Sir Walter, 1st Lord Aston, taught his family the new religion, and in 1642, Walter, 2nd Lord Aston is listed as a Roman Catholic Landowner who took arms for King Charles I.[38]

Daniel Bayley, Rector in 1648, was one of 5 incumbents whose livings were sequestered by Oliver Cromwell's Parliament but who subsequently acted as ministers during the interregnum in small villages, where it is possible they may have continued to use the Prayer Book, although this was forbidden.

Daniel Bayley had been married at Haughton on August 28th 1627 and became Rector at St Mary's, Stafford in 1639.

It appears that he was transferred from St Mary's to Tixall by Parliament in 1648 for "not having taken the covenant". He was restored to St Mary's c1661, but retained his living at Tixall until his death c1676.[32]

In 1660 the Anglican Church was re-established, and two years later a revised Book of Common Prayer was published, and is still used at Tixall.

Ralph Phillippes became Rector of Tixall on the death of Daniel Bailey in 1676. He was already minister and living at Tixall in 1666, when he is registered as having 4 hearths in the Tixall Constablewick for the Staffordshire Hearth Tax.[39]

In comparison Walter, 2nd Lord Aston had 34 hearths, William Launder had 4, and William Handsacre had 3. Five others including John Preston, Churchwarden, had 2 hearths; and another 5 including James Beresford, Churchwarden, had 1 hearth, giving a total of 60.

The earliest known reference to a burial at Tixall is in the will of Richard James, 1617, which says that his body is to be buried at Tixall,[40] previously all burials had been at St Bertelin's, Stafford.[1]

This is explained by a reference c1675, "The Church here ,*ie. in Tixall* (now reputed a parish church) was formerly a prebend belonging to the Collegiate Church in Stafford, But ye lords of ye manor had ye advowson as is evident from the fine recited. The Rectory is valued in ye King's books at £8 - 0s - 8d.[41]

In 1676 when Ralph Philips was Rector, the Church living is described as follows:-[42]

"Little ould orchard, a hempbut, a garden lying 10yds round ?
A little meadow below the hempbut
4 days work of wheat land lying in the field called the high clay
3 days work or thereabout in ye? middle field in 4 sou..? all
                                                                    places
A leasow about 5 acres? adjoining to Ingestre ...
A ...? lately taken in called by the name of ox pasture about
                                                                    acres
½ of a little meadow called the Hollie meadows
½ a days math (*mowing*) in Hollis ford meadow
4 acres? or thereabout called the pool field leasow"

This shows that fields in Tixall c1676 were in the process of being enclosed,eg. "lately taken in by the name of Ox Pasture about 13 acres."

The reference to "3" and "4 days work" suggests fields still unenclosed, with the Rector having as much as could be ploughed in 3 and 4 days respectively.

It is not until 1762 that all the Rectors fields are enclosed.

In 1682 the Rectory is described as[43] :-
House containing 5 bays
2 barnes containing 5 bays
2 little gardens & 1 croft adjoining house
                                                containing 1 acre

This suggests that the Rectory was a timber framed building with 5 bays or sections.

In 1682 Tithes were paid of "Corn, Hay, Wool, Lamb, Hemp, Flax, Pig, Goose & Apples - all in proper kinds, except for my Lord Aston's Demesne for which he pays £10 p.a."

This means that Lord Aston paid £10 pa in lieu of paying tithes for the lands which he farmed himself.

Regulations were later introduced to ensure that the Churches Tithe portion was chosen at random, and so was not the smallest or worst ! Hence in 1735, the 3rd goose and pig in every 7 is chosen, and the 10th bundle of Hemp & Flax.[44]

It also appears that Rectors had been overrun with Tithe milk & calves and so these tithes had been converted to cash payments :-

"The Tithe Hay & Corn in kind of all the parish
                                except the Demesne £10 pa
Apples & pears are paid in kind
Geese & Piggs the third in seven
for the Tith milk of every a cow 1 penny
& ½d for a calf and if 7 a crown
Hemp & Flax the 10th bundle"

Edward Wetenhall, who later became Bishop of Cork, and later Kilmore, was born at Tixall in 1678.[45] He died in 1713 and was buried at Westminster Abbey.

3. STEPHEN DUGDALE'S EVIDENCE AGAINST THE TIXALL GROUP OF CATHOLICS 1678 - 1680

In 1673 an Act was passed banning anyone who would not take Anglican Communion, eg. Catholics, from holding any public office.

Walter 3rd Lord Aston, the third Roman Catholic Aston, was sent to the Tower alongwith his friend Lord Stafford, in 1680 as part of the Titus Oates Plot, having been incriminated by his agent Stephen Dugdale.

Titus Oates believed that a wide-spread plot was on foot to murder the King, place the Duke of York on the throne, and establish the Catholic Religion in England.[46] In fact there was no such plot, only a conspiracy to re-introduce the Roman Catholic Religion to England.

Stephen Dugdale[47]

When his father died, Walter 3rd Lord Aston, had discovered some irregularities in the estate accounts, including a £300 fraud, and had either dismissed his bailiff, Stephen Dugdale, or the latter had absconded.

Dugdale was addicted to gambling, and had often withheld wages due to labourers and other workmen.[3]

There would have been no banks as we know them at this time, and the income from the estate was probably kept in a large locked chest, with the steward or bailiff having the key.

Oates had been looking for witnesses to support his accusations for three months, and when Dugdale was arrested soon after leaving Tixall Hall he appeared an ideal candidate.

At first Dugdale swore he knew nothing of any plot. He was left in Stafford Gaol for a few days, and then the possibility of a free pardon for all his offences and a reward were suggested, if he could provide suitable evidence for Oates.

On Christmas Eve, 1678, Dugdale gave his first information on the Tixall group of Catholics:-

" Whilst Harcourt [the Provincial of the Jesuits in England] was copying something in the house of Lord Aston, I had the opportunity," he affirmed on oath, " of observing his handwriting.

I next saw a letter which was written in his own hand, and was sent by the public letter-carrier to Every or Evers, a Jesuit [the chaplain at Tixall] instructing him to depute trusty and daring men — whether noblemen or commoners mattered not— to kill the King.

I was very often present at deliberations on that affair, held in Every's chamber, when Gavan [a priest of Wolverhampton] delivered an address to the assembly, grounded upon divine matters of Scripture, which I do not remember, proving both the lawfulness and excellence of this action, and I was solicited to undertake the business myself.

After this, I drew 600 gold crowns and received the promise of another 400 to accomplish the work.

Gavan thereupon assured me that, in return for my services, I should be enrolled in the Calendar of Saints.

Turner, [who voluntarily surrendered himself as a Jesuit] two years ago, in Every's chamber, plotted the death of the King, and undertook to promote the affair in Worcestershire.

I saw a letter from Waring [Jesuit Rector of London, afterwards executed on this information] dated October 4, 1678, in which these words were distinctly written 'This

-22-

evening Justice Godfrey is despatched.'

When Dugdale was examined before the King in Council in February 1679 he "brocaded his original affidavits with picturesque and imaginative details.":-

" The informant" wrote the Clerk "saith that he hath before, in discourse, acquainted the Lords of the Committee that, while he was in prison in Stafford and before he came to make his confession, there was much discourse spread abroad that he would confess.

Upon which report, Elizabeth Elde was sent over by Lord Aston to Mr Fitter, the priest of Mr Fowler at St Thomas, desiring him to have a meeting with his Lordship in a certain field called Brancote, near the River side, which was done accordingly. *(Thomas Loxdale, Rector of Tixall in 1719 married Elizabeth Eld, probably the daughter of Francis Eld of Seighford Hall in the 1700's -was this the same Elizabeth or a relative ?)*

When Fitter came home he told one of Mr Fowler's daughters what had passed, "hearsay once removed, " namely, that they, discoursing of the informant and of the danger of his discovering [ie. disclosing] all, Lord Aston did even weep, and that Fitter did tell his lordship he suspected that the informant would prove untrue, and that his lordship had done ill that he did not despatch him before ever ever he [Dugdale] went out of his house.

This discourse Mr Fowler's daughter told to Elizabeth Elde, " hearsay twice removed, " she being a messenger of trust employed to bespeak the said meeting.

And Elde did come to the informant while he was in prison at Stafford, which is but two miles from Tixall from which he had some messenger every day, and did relate the whole matter to him." That is hearsay thrice removed, Dugdale himself making the fourth medium through which the story had filtered in its journey to its present audience.

. " He further saith that, after that, he made his discovery [disclosure] .

Thereupon the Justices issued warrants for the seizure of George Hobson and George North (which North is nephew to Pickering) both of them servants in the house of the Lord Aston.

The warrants were served by Edward Preston, the constable of the place, and also a servant to the said lord."

There were several reports that Lord Aston had said:
"that he was sorry he had not run the informant through with his sword before he went out of the house."

Dugdale's evidence continued:-
" He did repeat this story to Joseph Tarboy, another of Lord Aston's servants, who came to see him in prison.
Informant bid him tell his lordship that he was sorry Lord Aston should have any thoughts to do him such injury.
The next day Tarboy returned to the informant, having with him the constable, Preston, to testify that his lordship did send him word that he never wished the informant's finger to ake, but wished him all happiness he could imagine, and hoped all would do well and that the informant might come back to his service."

Unfortunately, Sir William Bagot, the Staffordshire magistrate, swore that Lord Aston had disowned his late bailiff with the words:
" He is no servant of mine."

As a result of all this information, Lord Aston was impeached and committed to the Tower.

Father Evers, Chaplain of Tixall, managed to escape to the Continent after a number of hairbreadth escapes.

Father Gavan of Wolverhampton was arrested in London, hiding in the coachman's bed in the stables of Count Woleysteyn. He asked to be tried by the obsolete but still legal method of trial by ordeal, but neither this nor his ably conducted defence could save him.

Lord Stafford who had been imprisoned at the same time as Lord Aston, was nearly seventy years old, and "it would be difficult to imagine one less inclined by temperament to indulge himself in treason or conspiracy."[46]

According to Reresby, "He was deemed to be weaker than the other lords in the Tower, and was therefore purposely marked out to be the first brought on [to trial]."

At the trial of Lord Stafford which started on November 30th, 1678, Dugdale gave the following evidence to the House of Lords:-[47]

Lord Stafford[3]

" I have been frequently aquainted, while I was a servant at my Lord Aston's, with my Lord Stafford coming to my Lord's house in the country.

And, my Lord having been there several times, I came to such intimacy, by Mr Evers' *(the chaplain)* means, that my Lord would frequently discourse with me.

About the latter end of August or some day in September, my Lord Aston, my Lord Stafford and several other gentlemen, were in a room in Lord Aston's house and by means of Mr Evers, I was admitted to hear for encouragement.

And there I heard them fully determine that to take the life of the King *(Charles II)* was the best way they could resolve on as the speediest means to introduce their own religion.

Sometime in September, my Lord being at Mr Abnett's house in Stafford, my Lord Stafford came to Tixall upon a Sunday to hear Mass.

I meeting him at the outer gate as he alighted from his horse, he said to me, it was a sad thing they could not say their prayers but in a hidden manner; but ere long we should have our religion established.

After that my Lord Stafford was sometimes at Stafford and sometimes at Tixall.

I will not be positive to a day, but I think about the middle of September he sent to me to come to his lodging, I think by his page or him that waited upon him in his chamber.

> He was arising and dressing.
>
> He sent his men out and with many fair speeches offered me £500 to kill the King."

This confirms that a Roman Catholic Chaplain was living at Tixall Hall and celebrating the catholic mass there.

Dugdale also alleged that he heard treasonable conversation when he was standing concealed behind an oak tree at Tixall. This was the large spreading oak by Tixall Bowling Green, which had a shed with seats.[3] The bowling green was destroyed around 1787, but the oak was still standing in 1908 and was known as "Stafford's Oak".

Lord Stafford called Sir Thomas Whitgreave, who attested that Dugdale, when first arrested, had resolutely denied the existence of any plot at all.

Other witnesses swore that Dugdale had offered them heavy bribes to give evidence against the prisoner.

Lord Stafford's evidence was as follows:

He had been staying at Tixall in September as on the 21st was the great footrace at Etching Hill, nearby. Running Footmen were hired at these races and he was looking for a runner for Lord Danby.

On that morning:-

> "I was in my bed, and my servant (with me 12 or 14 years) told me Stephen Dugdale dared not ask to go to the race, because my Lord Aston was angry with him for meddling in races.
>
> Would I get leave for him ?
>
> I was not overwilling.
>
> I knew Lord Aston would not refuse me, but he might perhaps take it ill to be asked. But I sent for Dugdale and asked him some questions - who would win, etc.
>
> I promised to ask leave for him to go and I asked Lord Aston for him to go with my servant to show him the way.
>
> Dugdale stayed in the room while I dressed.
>
> We were not alone one moment together."

The trial lasted 6 days and Lord Stafford was found guilty of high treason by a majority of 24. He was executed at the Tower on December 29th 1680.

At his execution he said of Oates, Turbervile and Dugdale:
" All the punishment I wish them is that they repent and acknowledge the wrong that they have done me. God forgive them ! ... I do with my last breath assert my innocency, and hope the omnipotent, all-seeing, just God will deal with me accordingly." [47]

William, Lord Aston's brother, was also taken into custody because he refused to give evidence about a wallet, said by Dugdale to have been in the chaplain, the Rev.Evers closet. [3]

In June 1685, following the death of Charles II, Walter 3rd Lord Aston was discharged from the Tower " on application to Parliament", and Titus Oates was tried for perjury on May 9th 1685.

Walter Chetwynd of Ingestre was an ardent active-catholic who believed totally Titus Oates' fabrication of the Popish Plot to murder the king.

As MP for Stafford, he had raised angry questions in Parliament when Stephen Dugdale's evidence against Lord Stafford had been doubted at the trial.

When Walter Chetwynd was shown to have been wrong, he had to seek permission from Parliament to go into the country to recover his health. [48]

Mr William Ireland, a Roman Catholic Priest had been executed for high treason in 1678 on the oath of Titus Oates.

At the trial of Titus Oates, Lord Aston and his nephew gave evidence that Mr Ireland was not in London when Oates said he had seen him, and it is interesting to note the extensive travels of Lord

Aston's household:-[3]

> August 1678: Ireland went to Lord Aston's house at Standon, Herts.
>
> 5th August: Ireland & Lord Aston met Sir John & Lady Southcote (his sister) in St Albans with their sons, and they all went to Tixall.
>
> 15th August: They all went to Holywell with the Dowager Lady Aston *(Presumably to visit St Winifred's Well)*
>
> 16th August: All returned to Tixall
>
> 1st September: Ireland went to Mr Gerard's at Hilderstone
>
> 8th September: Ireland returned to Tixall
>
> 9th September: Ireland returned with Sir John Southcote to Surrey

Oates was found guilty; fined 20000 marks; stood twice at the pillory; publicly whipped twice; and imprisoned for life.

4. SIMON WAKELIN: RECTOR 1680 - 1698.

Simon Wakelin provides the earliest physical link with the present church, although in fact the building he knew was two rebuilds before the present one. He was the nephew of Sir Simon Degg.

A white marble oval memorial in the north aisle inscribed in Latin bears his name:-

M.S.
SIMONIS WAKELIN
GVLIELMI WAKELIN de VTOXETER
et DOROTHEAE UXOMS
Fily unici
Artium Magutri Rectorisq
hujus Ecclefiae
Cui (praeter beneficia quae contulerat vivus)
moriens patinam calicemq argenteum
Vico vero de VTTOXETER (natah fuo)
perpetuos fundi cujusdam fui reditus
ad ufum pauperum
reliquit
Obijt 23 die Martis Ao DOM
MDCXCVII
Aetatis fuae
38

ie. To the menory of Simon Wakelin,
only son of William Wakelin of Uttoxeter and Dorothy his wife,
the Rector of this Church, to which, besides other benefactions in his lifetime, he
left at his death a paten and a chalice of silver.
Died 23rd March 1697 aged 38.

This is no doubt the result of the £50 left in his will for a memorial, although he had asked to be buried near the altar.(See below)

In 1817, Clifford records "Against one side of the chancel is an oval monument of white marble ..."

The memorial was probably moved to the north aisle when the Church was rebuilt in 1848.

Tixall Church still uses the small Communion Cup given to Simon by his mother in 1689, which is inscribed:-
"The gift of Dorothy Wakelin, Mother of Simon Wakelin Rector to the Church of Tixall May the 24th 1689."

It is 6" high, weighs 5¼ozs, and has a beaker shaped bowl with a curved lip on a truncated stem with a central knob and rounded foot with a flat edge.

It was made in London by JA in 1688.

Simon Wakelin wrote a will dated March 1st 1697[49]:-

- My body to be buryed in the Chancell of my pish Church of Tixall under or near the holy Alter or Communion table at the discretion of my Executor.

(Cont.)

- & I leave the sum of £50 to be laid out on a monument at the oversight and appointment of my good friends Matthew Draksford, Rector of Stafford & James Millnos, Rector of Ingestre.

- to my dear mother Dorothy Wakelin *(50 Struck through)* 5 & all interest in parcel of land called the Picknall lately purchased off Richard Minors - joint with my father and myself.

- Cousins John & Edward £30 a p.....
      Samuel their brother £5
     & to William son of Thomas Wakelin of Loxby £20 because of the abuse of his faith to him.
- Land at Uttoxeter to cousins there and then to the poor of Uttoxeter.

- My Silver Salvor & Three Silver Castors *(vessels used to contain condiments at table)* to be wrought or exchanged into a silver sloope or flagon for the use of the Church of Tixall forever at the discretion & appointment of the said Matthew Draksford & James Millnos
- the said salvor to continue in the present form
& I leave a Diaper Cupboard Cloth for the use of the Communion Table of the said Church

& I leave to Matthew Draksford & James Millnos any books they have not already.

- Anything left me by my mothers relations or given me to be returned to children or nearest relations excepting Simon .... & my Aunt Pratt, this to be done at the discretion of my mother.

- I leave to the said Aunt Pratt £3 to buy herself mourning apparrell.

- John Warnor of Bromshill - all monies of mine he hath at present in his hands.

- & to Mary Clark, sister of Waltor Wakelin I do not particularly leave anything, yet my will is that my Executor show himself kind to her, especially if she comes to want.

- remainder left to Waltor Wakelin of Radbourne, Derby - my beloved coz.

The large paten and chalice donated at his death are kept at the Lichfield Heritage Centre Treasury.

The paten weighing 12¾ozs, is engraved " S * W "on the back, and was made by William Gamble in London in 1697.

The large chalice, 9¼" high and weighing 26ozs, is engraved:-
"ECCLESIAE de TIXHALL
ex dono SIMONIS WAKELIN Rectoris Ao Dom 1689".
It was made in London by GA in 1700 of Brittania Silver.

On December 3rd, Simon Wakelin had a violent nose bleed, and the Apothecary was called to let blood.

He then made some alterations to his will, reducing his mother's bequest from £50 to £5, and adding that Barbara Ryley should have nothing from him " she having gone away and left him unhandsomely in his sickness."

According to his memorial stone he died on March 23rd 1697, but an Inventory of his possessions is dated March 13th 1698[49].(See page 33 and 34)

It is interesting that he appears to have 25 chairs, 6 stools and 4 tables, but only one chest of drawers and there is no mention of cupboards.

INVENTORY OF SIMON WAKELIN'S POSSESSIONS
March 13th 1698

In the Chamber over the Great Parlour
      one bed & furniture 9 cane chairs
      one table & looking glass -------------------------------£20
In the Chamber over the Kitchen
      one bed & furniture 2 chairs
      2 stools 1 trunk 1 forestose? & 1 close stoole ---------£10
In the Chamber over the Little Parlour
      one bed & furniture -------------------------------------£1
In the Great Parlour
      2 tables 12 chairs 1 chest of drawers 1 looking glass £5
In the Little Parlour
      one bed & furniture & 1 stoole -------------------------£2
In the Buttery
      Barrells & Bottles -------------------------------------£2
In the Kitchen
      A furnace & brewing vessells --------------------------£2 - 10 -
      1 table, 2 chairs & 2 stools-------------------------   - 9 -
      A Jack Iron work and Crafs ? Pewter ------------------£7
      Plate--£5
      Linnen ---£2
In the Barne
      A Malt? Mill ---£1
      Corn thresh & unsettled ?-------------------------------£5
Without Doors
      2 Cows & 1 Sterk --------------------------------------£8
      His Horse ---£3
      Manure ---   10/-
      Hay ---£5

      His Purse, Apparrell & Books--------------------------£15
      Lumber & small things not particularly mentioned--   10/-
      Money due upon bonds---------------------------------£30
                                         £124 - 15

The brewing vessels appear to be the most important item in the kitchen. As the Rector had access to both apples and wheat, and had a malt mill in his barn, he could have made both cider and beer.

Diagram to show possible relative positions of rooms, etc. at Tixall Rectory in 1698.

CHAMBER Bed & Furniture 9 cane chairs Table Looking Glass	CHAMBER Bed & Furniture 2 Chairs 2 stools 1 trunk 1 close stool	CHAMBER Bed & Furniture	STABLE	BARN
GREAT PARLOUR 2 tables & 12 chairs Chest of drawers Looking Glass	KITCHEN Furnace & Brewing Vessels Table, 2 chairs & 2 stools	LITTLE PARLOUR Bed & Furniture Stoole		
	BUTTERY Barrels & Bottles	HOLDYARD		

BARN 2 bays	

5. TIXALL CHURCH IN THE 1700's & THE CHURCH REBUILT IN 1772

It can be assumed that at in the early 1700s Tixall Church would have been a small stone building.

As the local landlord, Lord Aston was a Catholic alongwith most of his servants, the Anglican Church at Tixall would have received little support, financial or otherwise, except for the fees taken for weddings, etc.

Hence in 1722:-[50]
Wedding with licence 5/-
Wedding without licence 2/6
Churching & Registering 1/-
    & the same for a buryall except they come out of
    another parish & then the Fee is double

And in 1732 the surplice dues are given for both the parson and the parish clerk[51]:-
Wedding with licence 5/- to the parson
    "   2/6 to the clerk
Wedding with Banns 2/6 to the parson
    "   1/-   to the clerk
Registring & Christening 1/- to the parson
    "   6d to the clerk
Burial 1/- to the parson
    " 2/- to the clerk

Presumably the higher burial fee for the parish clerk was because the clerk had to arrange for the grave to be dug, or even dig it himself.

In 1735 there is an additional fee of 1/- for the parson from publishing banns.[44]

There were 4 different Rectors appointed in the 1700's (See page 9). The first Thomas Holbroke, son of the Rector of Edgmond, was Rector from 1707 for 28 years.

According to his successor Thomas Loxdale, Holbroke destroyed all the early parish registers[3] and therefore the current registers start at June 7th 1707.

Thomas Loxdale was born on October 3rd 1675 in Meretown in the parish of Forton, where his family had held a copyhold estate since the early 16th century.

Printed sources give him three different fathers including Joseph[52] and John Loxdale.[53]

He was assistant curate at Forton from 1698 until 1703 when he was made Vicar of Seighford.

He was presented to the Rectory of Tixall in 1719 and moved there soon after. The following year, 1720 he married Elizabeth Eld, the daughter of Francis Eld of Seighford Hall.

Their only child, Thomas was born, and baptised at Tixall on February 17th 1722, but died of smallpox at Leek in 1729 and was buried at Seighford.

He remained Rector of Tixall until his death in 1742.

He resigned from Seighford in 1723, and from 1725 to 1735, he was Vicar of Leek as well as being Rector of Tixall.

While he was Vicar of Leek he had a succession of Curates looking after Tixall, including John Robinson who later became Vicar of Milwich.

The Parish Register records:-
August 3rd 1733 David son of John Robinson, Clerk baptized.
September 2nd 1733 David son of John Robinson, Clerk buried

In 1735, when Thomas Loxdale was 60, he retired to Tixall and remained there until his death. He was buried at Seighford next to his son on April 21st 1742.

His will dated 22nd January 1740,[54] (granted probate on May 20th 1742) left his wife a yearly annuity of £10 for the house at Stafford, my Quarto Bible & any other books out of my study that she shall chuse; £50 to his brother James; £5 to his couz Eliz Thorley; £20 to his sister Esther Saunders; £20 to his nephew Thomas son of Joseph for his education, and a silver tankard; 1 guinea to the current servant maid; and the remaining books, bonds, clothes, etc. to his brother Joseph, sole executor.

The nephew, Thomas was Mayor of Shrewsbury in 1774, so the money for his education appears to have been well spent.

Thomas Loxdale was described by the Rector of Forton, Rev. Samuel Du Gard, as" a man of great learning and piety", and was a keen local historian with an extensive collection of manuscripts.

On May 20th 1742, the Chancellor, Masters and Scholars of the University of Oxford " the true and undoubted Patron for This Turn of the Rectory of the Parish Church of Tixall ... now vacant by the natural death of the late Rector thereof ... present Ralph Turner MA"as Rector.[55]

On August 3rd 1742, Sir Walter Wagstaff Bagot of Blithfield: "being the true and undoubted Patron in full right of the Rectory and Parish Church of Tixall .... present John Robinson BA Clerk to the Rectory .... being now void by the death of Thomas Loxdale, Clerk, the last incumbent".[56]

Maybe this was an unsuccessful attempt by the friends of John Robinson, who had been the Curate and lived at Tixall Rectory while Thomas Loxdale was Vicar of Leek.

In any case Ralph Turner was appointed to the living. He was married to Elizabeth and the following children of theirs were baptised at Tixall:-

Ralph on February 15th 1753
Thomas on January 29th 1754

Elizabeth on February 20th 1755
William on October 27th 1758

Two years after the baptism of William, Ralph died (probate was granted December 27th 1760).[57] His goods were to be divided between his children, and " examine all my papers and to burn such as are not of any real value". His wife and brother John, and Richard Fenton of Breewood, Clerk were his executors.

Ralph was succeeded by William Corne, and it is recorded in the Parish Register that on March 8th 1761:-

"William Corne Clerk MA did read morning and evening Prayer and also the 39 articles together with the Bishops Certificate &ᶜ in the Parish Church of Tixall and made such declaration as the law in that case requires.

In the hearing of us   Mitford Wilkinson
Wm Clegg "

William Corne was the son of another Rev.William Corne, and had been born in Stafford in 1737. He matriculated at Trinity College, Oxford on March 23rd 1753, obtaining his BA in 1756 and his MA in 1759.[58]

His father died in November 1753 aged 57, and is commemorated by a plaque high in the North Transept of St Mary's, Stafford.

Four of William Corne's children were baptised at Tixall:-
1. September 6th 1761 - Thomas, son of
                    William Corne, Rect.& Mary
2. June 1st 1771 - Ellen daughter of
                    Wm Corne, Rector & Helen
3. October 16th 1773 - Elizabeth daughter of
                    Wm Corne, Rect. & Helen
4. September 6th 1775 - William son of
                    Wm Corne, Rect. & Ellen

In 1767, while William Corne was Rector, the Banns between Francis Yates of St Mary's, Stafford, and Mary Barker of Tixall, were forbidden at the 2nd reading on August 30th — perhaps they were underage.

William's memorial in the North Transept of St Mary's, Stafford, records :-

Sacred
to the Memory
of the Rev William Corne MA
Rector of Tixall & Swinnerton
Both in this County
of the former parish he was incumbent sixty
and of the latter ten years
He died October 18 1822 in the 88th year of his age
Also in memory
of Mary first wife of the Rev.William Corne
who died November 2 1768
Also of Helen
Second wife of the Rev.William Corne
who died February 1 1813 aged 66 years
also of Elizabeth
younger daughter of the above
William and Helen Corne
who died March 29 1801 aged 27 years
also of Helen
eldest daughter of the above
William and Helen Corne
who died June 29 1833 aged 62 years

He had married Ellen Peake (Helen) of St Thomas's (being extra-parochial & adjoining this parish) by licence on 27th February 1770, at Tixall.

In 1776 William Corne's Rectory was described as:-[59]

" A Parsonage house with a brewhouse adjoining and a granary over it.

A barn adjacent to the Brewhouse with a rickyard east of it.

A foldyard lying southward in which stand 2 stables, a Cowhouse, a Cart house and a Pig Stye.

A garden contiguous to and lying on the east, north and west sides of the house.

Adjacent to the garden eastward lies a croft containing about 1½ acres.

At the distance of about a mile to the north-east and contiguous to each other lie 8 fields viz. the cote leasow, the cote meadow, the middle field leasow, the middle field meadow, the salt clods and the 3 ox pastures, the whole containing about 32 acres.

Tythe in kind both great and small of the whole Parish except the Demesne which pays a yearly modus of £10 at Michelmas and Lady Day."

In 1786 a further stable had been made to give a total of 3 stables. [60]

On December 13th 1792, Mary Clifford *(Daughter of Barbara Aston & the Hon. Thomas Clifford)* married Charles Wolesley of Wolseley Hall, Colwich. William Corne took the service at Tixall Church, and the witnesses were:

Thomas Clifford *(Brother of the Bride)*
Mary & Edward Blount *(Aunt & Cousin of Bride)*
Mary McDonnell Clifford *(Wife of Thomas Clifford)*
Lucy Clifford *(Sister of the Bride)*

Since the 1753 Marriage Act, no one could be legally married except by a Church of England Parson, and hence the Catholic Cliffords had to have a ceremony in Tixall Church.

William Corne's youngest son, William became a minister himself. He matriculated at Christ Church, Oxford on May 30th 1793, obtained his BA in 1797 and his MA in 1800. In 1809 he was awarded his BD. [58]

He officiated at a marriage at Tixall on September 9th 1816, when he was described as William Corne jun[r].

In 1817 Clifford says:- [3]

" The present incumbent is the Rev. William Corne, who has been rector of Tixall, ever since the year 1760; and

though now above eighty years of age, is still in complete pos-
session of all his faculties.

He reads the smallest print without spectacles, which indeed he never uses.

He has an active mind, is a good scholar, and possesses a
retentive memory stored with various information and amus-
ing anecdotes, which he loves to communicate, and in a very
agreeable manner to those who enjoy the pleasure of his company."

The Rev. Corne died at the Rectory on October 18th 1822 aged
87.

It is interesting to note a different view of the Rev.William
Corne to that previously expressed by Clifford in 1817.

In 1833 the RC Chaplain of Tixall, the Rev.T.L.Green published
a 50 page booklet on correspondence between himself and the
Rev.William Webb, Rector of Tixall, concerning the burial of Roman
Catholics in Tixall Churchyard.[61]

In his introduction the Rev.Green says:-

"The late Parish Clerk died about 2 years ago at the
advanced age of 77 years (*Walter Malpas who died May 15th
1831*). He had been a servant in the family of the late Rector
upwards of 40 years; and had held the situation of Sexton and
Parish Clerk for nearly the same period. The Rector died in
the year 1822, having amassed in the course of his long Rec-
torship, a considerable property. He bequeathed the principal
part to an only daughter,*(Helen)* a maiden lady, in the neigh-
bourhood, lately deceased; but left his old faithful and well-
deserving servant entirely destitute.

The daughter, moreover, though applied to in his behalf,
was unwilling to contribute to his support; and had it not been
for the generous charity of the Catholic Proprietor of Tixall, he
must have passed the remainder of his days in abject poverty.
The present Sir Clifford Constable, from the time he was unable to earn a maintenance, granted him, a pension for life."

Helen Corne lived at The Hough, and when she died in June
1833, aged 62, the sale of her possessions took 3 days in the October.

The sale of the "choice and valuable library of books, chiefly selected by the late Rev.W.Corne, Rector of Tixall & Swinnerton" took the whole of the third day. The 460 books included:-[62]

History of Tixall
Franklin on Electricity
Natural History of England
Gages Survey of the West Indies
Voyage to New Holland in 1669
Newton on University Education
Switzer's gardeners recreation
Dampier's voyage round the world (2 vols)
Well's arithmetic
Art of Cookery
Millar's gardener's calendar
Blackstone's analysis of the laws of England
Wells treatise on mechanics & c
Patrick's geographia antiqua
Faick's essay on dropsy
Brooke's practise of physic (2 vols)
Toller's treatise on the law of tithes (3 vols)
Clarendon's history of the irish rebellion
Kent's hints to landlords
Potter's Mathematics
Reece's Medical Guide
Nature displayed (7 vols)
Echard's Roman History (5 vols)
Buccaniers of America 1699
Higgon's view of English History
Wells Astronomy & c
Duodecimo (123 vols)
Comic Songs
Surveyor
Sharpe's introduction to history (8 vols)
Blair's Geography
Theory of agreeable sensations
Bracken's Farriery (2 vols)
Historie de France
Brooke's Natural History (6 vols)
Classical Dictionary (2 vols)
Locke on Education

In 1772 the earlier small stone church was rebuilt.

T.P.Wood 1837   Tixall Church[63]

An account in 1871[64] says " the Parish Church of Tixall, dedicated to St John the Baptist, appears to have been rebuilt about a hundred years ago in a very plain style, and of less than its former dimensions."

There is some suggestion that only the chancel was totally rebuilt in 1772.[65] (See page   )

When this rebuild was taken down in 1848, "several fragments of stone tracery and mouldings were found embedded in the walls, showing that a church must have existed on this spot from very early times."

It is just possible that some of these fragments may have come from the Elizabethan Tixall Hall. In 1729, Richard Trubshaw had begun to "pluck down the East Front of Tixall",[66] presumably with the

? J.B.   NE View of Tixall Church 1841 [67]

Ground Plan of
TIXALL OLD CHURCH

intention of replacing it with a new one.

More work was carried out in 1738, and Richard's son Charles took over when his father died in 1745.

There is also reference to bricks being sent to Tixall Church in 1773, and men working there from February to July. Possibly these were for the brick floor.

The ground plan of the 1772 Church[68] shows it to have had an entrance under the tower at the west end, about 8 box pews with seating on both sides, and a further 8 single bench box pews.

The pulpit was on the right-hand side, and adjacent to it was

another small enclosed chamber, possibly a vestry with a separate entrance for the parson.

The font was in the south-west corner.

We have a sketch of this old font made by Mr Home on February 25th 1932.[69]

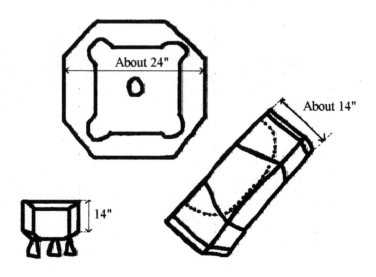

Mr Home continued:-

"Mr S.Dodd told me today that this font came out of Tixall Church when it was pulled down about 100yrs ago. He had the information from his father who was born about 1840.

The font is in front of the house at Tixall Heath - only the top remains which stands on 3 stone blocks."

Unfortunately it is no longer there now.

When the floor under the pews in the present church had to be taken up and excavated in December 1989 so that a new concrete base could be laid, I was able to carry out a very quick and cold trial excavation at the back of the church.

WEST WINDOW

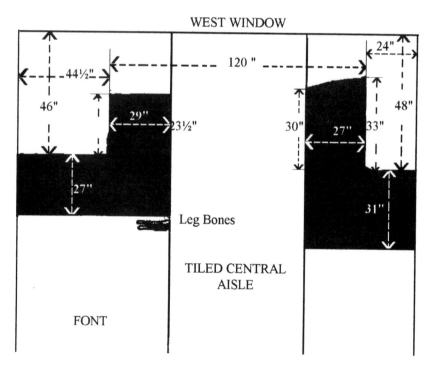

This showed the foundations of the west wall and tower base

of the earlier church within the present church.

The Aston's had remained Catholics, and would have continued to have their own private chapel within Tixall Hall.

James, 5th Lord Aston inherited Tixall in 1744 and a major rebuilding programme was started with the architect, William Baker of Audlem being paid 5 guineas for 5 days drawing plans on May 11th 1751, and a further guinea for "further advice" on May 24th.[70]

Unfortunately James died on August 20th 1751 leaving the work unfinished, but Charles Trubshaw submitted an account to his estate for work done in 1751 and 1752 and this appears to have included a chapel, no doubt within the hall.

Certainly in 1791 a chapel was registered for Roman Catholics by the Catholic Priest, George Beeston.[71]

George Beeston died August 15th 1791 aged 62, "having discharged the duties of Chaplain to the Family at Tixall Hall and Minister to the Catholic congregation there during thirty five years" ie. since 1756.

He was buried in Tixall Churchyard and his gravestone records:-
" He was righteous before GOD walking in all the commandments and ordinances of the LORD without blame."

6. TIXALL CHURCH IN THE EARLY 1800's

The Rt.Hon Viscount Granville, M.P. for Stafford, rented Tixall Hall for 8 years from 1810 to 1818. During this time two of his children were baptised at the parish church:-

October 10th 1812 - Georgiana Charlotte daughter of
        Lord Granville Levison and Lady Harriet Levison Gower
13th November 1817 - William Henry Gower son of
        Granville Levison and Harriet,
        father's occupation given as Viscount Granville

In 1817, Mr Le Sage, a French emigrant and grand nephew of the "ingenious" author of Gil Blas was living in the village and acting as RC Chaplain.[3]

Gil Blas was a picturesque romance by Lesage in four volumes published between 1715 and 1735. "A presentation of life with its vicissitudes and recoveries" concerning the life of Gil Blas, the son of humble Spanish parents who aged 17, sets off with his mule for the University of Salamanca but gets waylaid. "Its moral is that life is not so bad after all, provided we make the best of it and profit by experience; and moreover that life as a rule makes man better."[72]

Henry le Sage died on May 4th, 1821 aged 58, having "for eleven years discharged the functions of Pastor to the Catholic Congregation at Tixall", ie. since 1810.

In the will of Teresa Ward,[73] who died April 11th 1817, and was the wife of the late Francis Ward, she refers to " A close stool and a dumb waiter with a chair and 3 cushions in Tixall Chapel which I give to Joseph Ward of Brancott.

In the same year the church of Tixall, built in 1772, is described as "a small fabric of stone, with a low tower, and a rectory"[5] or as "a

small neat edifice, calculated to contain about eighty persons.[3]
"The church is a rectory in the gift of the proprietor of the parish, and is endowed with about forty acres of glebe-land, lying all together at one extremity of the parish: more than two-thirds of which are protected from tithe, by a *modus (ie. money payment in lieu of tithe)* of 10 *l (ie.£)* ; of the rest the rector is entitled to the great and small tithes. The value of the living is estimated at between 200 *l* and 300 *l (ie. £)* a year."

Following the death of William Corne in 1822, on March 29th 1823, Thomas Walker was presented to the Rectory at Tixall by William Keen of Stafford. His appointment was endorsed by the Perpetual Curate of St Mary's, Stafford, H.Rathbone; the Vicar of Baswich, Joseph Ellerton; and the Curate of Castlechurch, Robert Anluzask.[74]

On April 13th 1826, the Parish Register records that Charles Chichester of this Parish married Mary Barbara Constable by Licence. Thomas Walker was the Rector officiating, and Clifford, *(Hugh 7th Lord Clifford of Chudleigh ?)* Clifford Constable *(Thomas Aston Clifford Constable, brother of the bride)* and George Clifford *(uncle of the bride)*, were the witnesses.

Mary Barbara was the daughter of Sir Thomas Hugh Clifford, who died in 1823, and Mary Macdonald Chichester of Arlington, Devon, her aunt and mother of Charles.

Charles was later a Captain in the Duke of Yorks own Rifle Corps.

Until the Catholic Emancipation Act was passed in 1829 Catholics could not accept a commission in the army, and Catholic Lords could not attend Parliament.

It is interesting to note that this important wedding was the only service recorded as being taken by the Rector, Thomas Walker. All other marriages, baptisms and burials between the death of William

Corne in 1822 and the arrival of William Webb in 1831 were taken by Curates.

In July 1826 Joseph Smith was licensed as Curate at Tixall, taking the Oaths and Declaration of Conformity on July 21st as he had been unable to be present on July 4th.[75]

He was to receive £80 per annum and the use of the Rectory, which was valued at £200 per annum. His application was endorsed by the Rector of Gratwich, and the Curates of Ipstones and Barlaston.

In 1827 there was a double wedding on September 27th with Sir Thomas Aston Clifford Constable marrying Mary Ann Chichester of Calverleigh Place, Devon, and Henry Arundell, Esq. of St Georges, Hanover Square, marrying Isabella Constable *(brother of Thomas Aston, and sister of Mary Barbara)*.

The Curate, Joseph Smith, took the service and each couple acted as witnesses for the other. No doubt this was a quiet official ceremony to complement the large Catholic Nuptial Mass, possibly held in the private chapel at Tixall.

In 1829, George Hodson, Archdeacon and Vicar of Colwich visited Tixall on July 13th as one of the earlier of the Visitations of the Archdeaconry of Stafford, 1829 - 1841.[76]

His report on the Benefice of Tixall was as follows:-

Nature: Rectory
Ecton: Living discharged — Clear yearly value £46 10s 0d.
Patron: Sir [Thomas Aston] Clifford Constable, Bart. (Ecton, Lord Aston)
Impropriator: [I] could not ascertain — arrangement [relative to tithes] said to exist between the Patron and the Rector

(Cont.)

CHURCH: Plain building with circular windows—single body, separated from chancel, by circular arch.

Number it will contain: About 100.

Accommodation for Poor: None specified, but there is room for any who attend.

Walls: That on the S.Side wants inspection.

Floor: Brick—even.

Windows: Good—open casements.

Doors: Double doors at W entrance.

Pulpit and Desk: Oak—good.

Books: The Prayer Book, in reading desk, needs repair.

Seats: In good order.

Galleries: None.

Organ: —————-

Font: There is one.

Chapels: None.

Benefaction Table: None.

Vestry: None.

Linen: Table cloth and Napkin.

Plate: Two Cups and a Paten—not well kept.

Chest for Papers: There is one.

Iron Chest for Register: At the Rectory.

Register: Only two vols besides those now in use: the oldest date 1707 - it is said that the older vols were destroyed by a former Rector—Revd Thomas Holbroke, early in the 18th century—see Topographical Account of Tixall by Sir T.Clifford and Mr Arthur Clifford,p75.

Porch: None.

Vaults: None.

Cleanliness: Attended to.

Damp: Very little at bottom of walls.

Dimensions: 36ft. 5in. by 16ft.8in.

CHANCEL: 14ft.2in. [by 16ft. 8in.] The Church being much dilapidated, was partially taken down, and re-built on a *smaller* extent, about 50 years ago. *(ie. in 1772)*

-51-

Table: Plain Oak.
Ornaments: None.
Repaired by whom: The Rector.

STEEPLE: Low square tower, surmounted Lead Cupola and Vane.
State of: Good externally.
Bells: Two—one out of order—woodwork said to need repair.
Clock: None.

CHURCHYARD:
Fence: On the E. and S. walls of the Rectory garden; and road leading to the Rectory. W. and N. a low wall, or bank belonging to the Parish. The garden wall, in an insecure state.
Gates: Good.
Drains: None—directed.
Graves: A few too near the wall.
Rubbish: Little.
Footpaths: None.
Cattle: The Curate's horse.

DIVINE SERVICE:
On Sundays: Morning Prayers and Sermon—Afternoon Prayers.
On other Days: None.
Sacrement: four times a year.
Communicants: About 10.
Catechism: Not in the Church.

INCUMBENT:
Name and Residence: Revd. Thomas Walker, Standon, Eccleshall.
If not resident: Not.
What duty he performs: None.
CURATE:
Name and Residence: Revd. Joseph Smith in the Rectory.
Licensed: Yes.
Salary: £80 and the house.   **If serving another Church:** None.

PARSONAGE: An old brick, rough cast, building, with two parlours and kitchen—four bedrooms, garret and lumbar rooms. Beer-house. A new one stated to have been promised by Sir C.Constable to the present Rector.

State of: Very much out of repair—especially the roof and ceilings.

Outbuildings: Granary, Stables, Coach-house, Cart sheds— some of them exceedingly out of repair.

INCOME:

Gross Value: About £200.

Glebe: 40 acres.

Surplice Fees: £1 per annum.

Easter dues and small payments: None.

Queen Anne's Bounty: The Patronage being in a Catholic family, it is difficult to ascertain the nature of the arrangement, subsisting between the Patron and present Rector. The latter is said to receive a fixed sum in lieu of Tithes, Glebe etc.(*In 1836, following the Tithe Commutation Act, all tithes were paid in money not in kind)*

Terrier: (*List of Church Property)* None that the Curate knows of.

SCHOOLS:

Sunday School: None — the children being all Catholics.

DISSENTERS: **Dissenters' School:** A Catholic Sunday School — about 20.

Dissenting Chapels: Catholic Chapel at Sir Clifford's [house].

POPULATION: About 100.

MISCELLANEOUS:

Monuments: None

Chandeliers, etc: None

Parochial Library: None

PARISH CLERK: Walter Malpass

Appointed by: The Rector.

Salary: £4 a year and burial fees.

CHURCHWARDENS: Mr John Cliffe.

ORDERS MADE: ['Done'.] The state of the South Wall, and of the Roof to be examined and necessary repairs performed. An open drain made all round to carry off the wet. Ivy etc to be removed from the walls and plinth. The Rectory garden wall secured. The Communion Plate repaired, and better preserved. The Clergyman's Prayer book repaired. Windows in Church and Belfry mended. State of Bells, and woodwork, connected with them examined and [where needful] repaired. 'Nothing done'.

The principal repairs, however, are wanted in the Rectory House and Offices, concerning which the Rector to be written to."

The poor state of the Church in 1829 was probably partly due to the absence of a resident Rector since the death of William Corne in 1822 at the age of 87.

In 1831, William Webb was appointed Rector. He had gained his BA from Trinity College, Cambridge in 1828, and received his MA in 1834.[58]

One can only hope that the repairs to the Rectory had been carried out by then.

William Webb remained at Tixall until his death on March 27th 1883 aged 76, when he had been Rector for 52 years. He was married to Maria, daughter of William and Elizabeth Morgan, and the baptisms of their children are recorded in the Church Register as follows:-

16th Dec.	1832	Mary Elizabeth Webb
18th Sept.	1834	Arthur Henry Webb
22nd May	1836	Francis William Webb
14th Feb.	1838	Walter George Webb
26th Mar	1844	William James Webb

The 1851 Census lists the occupants of the Parsonage House as:-

William Webb	Aged 44	Rector of Tixall	b.Castlechurch
Marian Webb	Aged 44	Wife	b Lichfield
Mary Webb	Aged 18	Daughter	b Tixall
Arthur Webb	Aged 16	Scholar at Home	b Tixall
Francis Webb	Aged 14	Scholar at Home	b Tixall
Walter Webb	Aged 13	Scholar at Home	b Tixall
William Webb	Aged 7	Scholar at Home	b Tixall
Elizabeth Morgan	Aged 74	Mother in Law, Annuitant	b Mansfield
Sarah Thompson	Aged 41	Cook	b Lichfield
Mary Leland	Aged 20	Housemaid	b Colwich
Fanny Wright	Aged 19	Nurse	b Abbots Bromley

By the time of the 1861 Census, only Walter and William remained at home with their parents, and presumably Elizabeth Morgan had died, as neither she nor the nurse are listed:-

Walter G.Webb	Aged 23	Unmarried	
William Webb	Aged 17	Scholar	
Sarah Thompson	Aged 50	Cook	
Mary Harrison	Aged 27	Housemaid	b Tixall

The marriage of Walter was obviously a matter of local concern as three years later on December 3rd 1864 the Staffordshire Advertiser reported:-[77]

Reception last Thursday Evening to W.G.Webb Esq. and his bride on visiting the Rectory for the first time since their marriage.

Really sumptuous tea in the schoolroom provided by the villagers -- Address of congratulations read by one of their number followed by a presentation of an elegant butter vase, with an appropriate inscription on the silver cover purchased by their united subscriptions.

Dancing concluded the evening.

By 1903, when Francis wrote his will, Walter had become a Colonel.[78]

Two of the sons, Arthur Henry and William James, followed their father to Trinity College, Cambridge, and then into the Church.

Arthur matriculated in 1853, and obtained his BA in 1857, followed by his MA.

He was Curate at Sheriffhales from 1857 to 1859 when he became Priest in Charge.

In 1864 he moved to become Curate at Wigan Parish Church, and in 1870 he became Vicar of Dalton, Lancs.[58]

On several occasions Arthur helped his father out at Tixall:-

On May 16th 1861 he conducted the marriage by licence of Daniel Colin Campbell, Gentleman of Bicton, nr Shrewsbury, to Maria Louisa Webb, a minor of Tixall Rectory whose father was George Webb, Gentleman; in the presence of Daniel Campbell, father - a merchant, William Webb, M.E.Webb and Agnes Campbell.

In addition he took the following services at Tixall:-

May 22nd 1859	Burial
April 29th 1860	Baptism
October 20th 1861	Read some banns;
March 20th 1866	Baptism
June 8th 1866	Baptism
July 3rd 1870	Baptisms
July 24th 1870	Baptism
March 18th 1875	Baby's burial
October 13th 1878	Baptism

William James matriculated in 1863, and obtained his BA in 1867 followed by his MA.

He went to join his brother as Assistant Curate at Wigan from 1867 to 1868, when he became Curate in charge of Bradwell, Derbyshire, where he was Vicar from 1870 to 1880.

He then moved to Alrewas, where he was Vicar until his death in 1890.[58]

He also helped his father out at Tixall:-
- Aug. 9th 1868   Baptism
- Feb. 1st 1870   Burial
- Sept. 7th 1881   Burial
- June 8th 1882   Wedding of George Stevens Webb, Widower, Labourer of Tixall son of George Webb, Labourer.

It is interesting to note that apart from this family help William Webb took all but 13 baptisms, (6 in the last 6 months of his life), 1 wedding and 11 burials, during the whole 52 years he served as Rector at Tixall -- very different to some of his predecessors.

The Webb Family in the early 1870s.   NRM, York
From the left:- Mary, Walter, Francis, Rev.William, Arthur, William, and Mrs Marian Webb[78]

Sarah Thompson served as Rectory Cook for over 30 years.

By the 1871 Census, the unmarried daughter Mary, had returned to live with her 64 year old parents:-

Mary Webb	Aged 38	
Sarah Thompson	Aged 60	Cook
Mary Harrison	Aged 37	Housemaid

The Rector's wife, Maria or Marion, died on March 12th 1881, according to her tombstone, although her burial is recorded as March 11th..

The 1881 Census lists the Rectory inhabitants as:-

William Webb, Widr	Aged 74	Rector	
Mary Webb	Aged 48		
Anne Wogan	Aged 52	Niece	b Stafford
Elizabeth Warner	Aged 37	Cook	b Checkley
Ann Hawkins	Aged 35	Housemaid	b Checkley

William Webb gave notice to quit his tenancy with Lord Shrewsbury on 27th September 1882 for March 25th 1883.

He took his last burial service on May 24th 1882, his last baptism on November 2nd 1882, and his last wedding on January 3rd 1883, although he had not been in Church to read the banns.

He died on March 27th 1883 and was buried at Tixall with his wife on March 31st.

7. FRANCIS WILLIAM WEBB 1836-1906

Francis William was the second son of William Webb, Rector of Tixall 1831 - 1883.

Although Francis did not go to Cambridge like his brothers Arthur and William, in August 1851 at the age of 15 he became a premium apprentice with the LNWR at Crewe under Francis Trevithick.[78]

Unlike the ordinary apprentices who were trained for only one job such as turners, fitters, etc.and were usually the sons of Crewe or other LNWR employees, Premium Apprentices came from wider social circles and geographical limits, and covered a wide range of skills.

They usually paid about £200 in instalments for the 5 year apprenticeship, with half going to the Apprentice Fee Account at Euston and half to the Crewe Mechanics Institute

They were paid normal trade apprentice rates, and could attend some day classes at the Mechanics Institute.

In 1856 Trevithick reported:-
"Frank Webb, draughtsman in his office, is out of his apprenticeship, and that he is an exceedingly respectable young man and his services are very valuable. Resolved that it be recommended to the Executive Committee to retain Webb's services at £2 a week wage."

Three years later at the age of 22 he had become Chief Draughtsman under John Ramsbottom and received a salary of £220 a year.

By 1864, 3 years later he had become works manager and his salary had increased to £600 a year. During this time he had helped set up the Bessemer Steel Plant at Crewe, and started his career as an inventor.

His first two inventions were the steel-headed rail and the curvilinear slotting machine.

Solid steel rails had proved too expensive in 1863 at £3,301 for a mile of double track compared to £1,879 for iron rails, this included the Royalty payments of £1 - £2/ton for the Bessemer process. Webbs steel headed iron rail made more efficient use of the available steel.

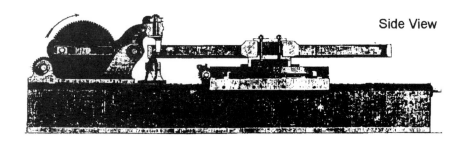

Side View

Plan View

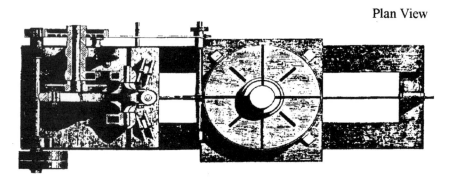

Webb's Curvilinear slotting machine of 1864[78]

Out of balance wheel rims produced unequal tread wear on the tyres of engine wheels. Webb's curvilinear slotting machine was devised to overcome this problem by machining the curved inner surface of the wheel rims between the spokes.

As Ramsbottom was only 52, Webb felt that there was little chance of further promotion at LNWR . Having 18 months experience at running a Bessemer Plant he became a manager at the Bolton Iron & Steel Co. for the Hick and Hargreaves families.

Four years later in 1870 Ramsbottom gave 12 months notice of his retirement due to stress, and his Works Manager, Thomas Stubbs died the same year.

Webb was contacted, and after a preliminary interview was sent the following letter dated 8th October 1870 by Sir Richard Moon, Chairman of the Company:-

" I took the opportunity as agreed of naming to our Special Committee what had passed with reference to your rejoining our Comp. as Locomotive Superintendent.

1st that the salary should be £2,000 for the 1st year and £3,000 afterwards. We thought that the notice had best be as in the case of Mr Ramsbottom, twelve months, and that the number of pupils if you take any, for your own comfort as well as ours, should be limited to four.

You know the regulations of the Co. as to patents and other matters, so that I need not trouble you with them here.

I do not know what rent Mr Ramsbottom pays for his house, but you can have it on the same terms as he had it.

I mentioned to the Committee that you could not leave the friends with whom you are at present for about 6 months, but that you may possibly arrange to leave then at an earlier period. We shall be ready for you whenever you can make arrangements to join us, and perhaps you will let me know after seeing your friends.

The Special Committee unanimously agreed to my proposal, and Mr Chance, the Chairman of the Locomotive Committee desired me to say that it has his special concurrence.

Hoping that you may have a long and promising career."

It was eventually agreed that Webb should leave Bolton and return to Crewe on June 30th 1871.

However, as Ramsbottom's notice had not yet expired and he was in slightly better health, it was decided that Webb should go on a short tour of the USA, at the LNWR's expense,to study steel making and locomotive practice.

He returned from the States in August and officially took over at Crewe on October 1st, where he remained in charge for over 30 years.

By 1901 he had designed and built 150 Compound Express Engines for the LNWR:-[79]

No. Built	Engine Class	HP Cylinders outside x2	LP Cylinders inside x1	Driving Wheels	Steam Pressure lbs
100 3-Cylinder Engines					
30	EXPERIMENT	13"	26"	6'6"	160
40	DREADNOUGHT	14"	30"	6'	175
10	TEUTONICS	14"	30"	7'	
10	GREATER BRITAINS	15"	30"	7'	
10	JOHN HICKS			6'	
50 4-Cylinder Engines					
50		15"	20.5" (x2)	7' (x4)	200

During this time production at Crewe increased steadily and covered a wide range of activities. These included steel and signal manufacture, a brickyard, gas plant, carriage works, and grease works.

Some parts of the works were 1 or 2 miles apart and hence Webb's close discipline was essential for smooth ad efficient running. However, the intense and complicated transfer of large and small parts within the works remained a problem.

The scale and range of engineering work is shown in the following table:-:-

Examples of Crewe Works Production while Webb was Chief Engineer[78]

Year	1870	1880	1890	1900	1903
New Locomotives built	69	93	70	100	95
Locomotives rebuilt, eg. new boiler	89	136	109	134	100
Locomotives cut up for steel	5	39	45	68	36
Locomotives sold	0	6	3	7	2
Locomotives given substantial repairs	1770	1477	1325	1257	1459
Locomotives painted	521	497	303	434	344
New tenders built	90	0	7	30	25
Tenders rebuilt - wooden frames	0	73	57	93	69
Tenders repaired	1092	1024	960	832	1039
Crank axles manufactured	211	218	106	218	234
New Boilers built	0	0	175	211	197
Boilers repaired	0	0	158	197	339
Average staff employed*	**4093**	**5617**	**6295**	**7376**	**7842**

* Excluding loco running, carriage repair, cleaning and storage.

A Webb 3-cylinder compound 2--2--2--2T of 1887
reputed to be the 3000th locomotive completed at Crewe works and bearing this special number plate for the photograph.[78]

Webb patented more than 75 inventions between 1864 and 1903, although many were not implemented or constructed.

While Sir Richard Moon was Chairman he favoured ordered economy and moderate schedule speeds for his locomotives as men and coal were cheap. This led to Webb having a policy of small engines for his first 20 years.

However, when Moon retired in 1891 Webb introduced larger 8--wheelers for top class passenger and freight services:-

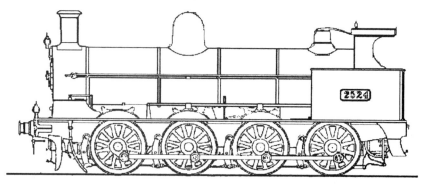

The first 8--coupled engine built at Crewe in 1892; simple expansion with two 19½in by 24in inside cylinders and 4ft 5½in wheels; weight 49 tons[78]

Webb "was of an autocratic and imperious disposition, and most of his staff were afraid of him, but he was nevertheless strictly just and honourable, and there are very many indications that his gruff exterior concealed a kind heart."[80]

He "was the undisputed 'King of Crewe' and throughout his reign no one--not even a director (with the possible exception of Lord Stalybridge, who was a personal friend) -- was allowed to visit Crewe Works without permission being sought and granted.
Some idea of the scale of his 'Kingdom' can be obtained from

the following plan showing the layout of shops at the Steeleworks end in 1889.[78] This was only part of the Crewe site.

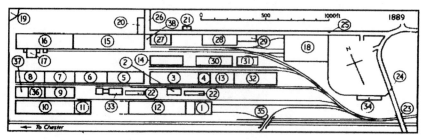

1. Steel Plant
2. Boiler House
3. Axle Forge
4. Spring Mill
5. No.5 Erecting Shop
6. No.6 Erecting Shop
7. No.7 Erecting Shop
8. No.8 Erecting Shop
9. Boiler Shop Smithy
10. Boiler Shop
11. Points & Crossings Shop
12. Steel Rail Mill
13. New or Iron Forge
14. Copper Shop
15. Tender Shop
16. Iron Foundry
17. Rail Chair Foundry
18. Paint Shop
19. Brickworks
20. Workman's Dining Room
21. Bessemer Hotel
22. Gas Products
23. Flag Lane Bridge
24. Flag Lane
25. Richard Moon Street
26. Goddard Street
27. Brass Foundry
28. Signal Shop
29. Signal Stores
30. Wheel Shop
31. Nut & Bolt Shop
32. Steel Foundry
33. Boiler House
34. Mortar Mill
35. Eagle Bridge
36. Flangeing Shop
37. Plate Stores
38. Works Entrance

Latterly, after Sir Frederick Harrison became General Manager of the LNWR in 1893, relations between 'Euston' and 'Crewe' became very strained, to a large extent, it is believed on good authority , because Webb's salary as Chief Mechanical Engineer was substantially higher than Harrison's as General Manager."[80]

" They were both self-opinionated men, and the younger

Harrison resented both Webb's independence of him and his much higher salary, for by then Webb was receiving £7,000 a year, at least 40% more than Harrison's salary."[78]

Bronze Bust of Francis William Webb
at Crewe Railway Museum

Webb belonged to many learned societies including:-[58]
The Iron & Coal Institute 1876
The Institute of Civil Engineering of France 1882
The Council of Civil Engineering 1888

He was also involved in public service, being made Mayor of Crewe from 1886-1888, and serving as a JP and Alderman on Cheshire County Council.

He was given the freedom of Crewe in 1900 when the 4,000th Crewe engine was completed.

He never married, but lived simply with a couple of servants at Chester Place, the company's house built in the early 1860s.

He enjoyed gardening, both there and at his country home,

Stanway near Church Stretton, where he went many weekends.

In November 1902, aged 66, Webb told the board he would soon have to retire.

The directors minuted:-

" Mr Webb having desired to be relieved from the duties of chief mechanical engineer, the directors wish to record their very great appreciation for the devoted and exceptional services he has rendered to the Company since his appointment in 1871."[78]

As has already been noted he had to give 12 months notice, and so it was not until April 1903 that his successor was appointed, and even then there was no mention of the official date for changeover.

After attending a few functions in May, Webb had to retire around the time of his 67th birthday.

According to one of the then Premium Apprentices:-

"   Webb had been one day away on business at Manchester, and on his return to his office in the late afternoon W.Horabin, then assistant chief clerk, brought in some letters for signature.

He thought Webb's usually abrupt manner had become rather peculiar, a feeling that changed to astonishment when Webb asked him if he he would like his overcoat.

Horabin managed to stammer out 'Well, sir, it would be a bit big for me,' for Webb was not far off 6ft and portly.

On getting outside Horabin reported to George Ellis, the chief clerk, and they sent a messenger to Webb's brother Canon A.H.Webb, at St Paul's vicarage.

The canon came over and persuaded Webb to go home with him, and the works did not see him again."[78]

Arthur Webb, Francis's brother, had been appointed to St Paul's Coppenhall, Crewe in 1879, and was Chaplain of the 2nd Cheshire Railway Volunteers, Royal Engineers, and an Honorary Canon of Chester Cathedral.[58]

Francis was taken seriously ill at the end of May in Colwyn Bay, recovered briefly but was then brought to Coton Hill mental hospital in Stafford.

After a few weeks he recovered sufficiently to buy a house in Bournemouth, where he remained until his death on June 6th 1906.

In his will dated 22 May 1903, before his breakdown, he left £211,542 a considerable sum in those days.[78]

Bequests included:-

£5,000 to Crewe Cottage Hospital;

£10,000 to found a nursing institution to give free attendance to the poorer people of Crewe;

£9,000 to various church purposes in Crewe;

Endowing a bed at University College Hospital, preferably for LNWR employees;

£1,000 to the men's convalescent home at Rhyl;

£1,000 to the Railway Servants Orphanage at Derby;

£2,000 to University College, Liverpool, and £2,000 to Owens College, Manchester; for scholarships for LNWR employees and their sons;

£1,000 to the Institution of Civil Engineers for Webb prizes for railway engineering papers;

£30,000 to his brother Canon A.H.Webb;

£30,000 to his brother Colonel W.G.Webb;

£5,000 to his nephew W.W.G.Webb an assistant at Crewe;

£5,000 to his friend Dr J.Atkinson of Crewe;

£5,000 to his friend G.R.Jebb of Birmingham;

£3,000 to his Crewe friend & solicitor A.G.Hill;

£5,000 to his godson Henry Robertson

£300 to George Ellis:

£200 to W.Horabin

The residue of about £70,000 went to found the Webb Orphanage at Crewe for the children of deceased LNWR employees.

8. The 1828 Catholic Chapel at Tixall Hall.

Thomas Clifford's new mansion built at Tixall in the 1780's had included a new chapel.[71]

His son, Walter had been educated in Liege at the Jesuit College, but had had to flee from there with his younger brother George, when the French drove them out in 1794.[81]

They had moved to Stoneyhurst, where Walter taught humanities and philosophy as an unordained junior ecclesiastic " a student, who for learning zeal and humility has not equal."[82]

Walter was ordained in 1801as a professed member of the Society of Jesuits, and celebrated his first mass at Tixall.

He died in July, 1806 in the Jesuit College at Palermo, Sicily where he had gone for the recovery of his health following breaking a blood vessel due to overwork. He was only 33.

In 1827, Thomas Clifford's grandson Sir Thomas Clifford, commissioned Joseph Ireland to build a new chapel at Tixall Hall. This was the first time that Roman Catholics were allowed to have a free-standing chapel.

The chapel adjoining the south wing of Tixall Hall and behind Tixall Gatehouse, was completed the following year.

It was registered at the Michaelmas Sessions in 1837 by the priest, T.L.Green, as "a separate building situate near the mansion house of Sir Thomas Aston Clifford Constable, baronet," for Roman Catholics.[83]

It is shown in situ in a contemporary painting:-

Tixall Chapel behind the Gatehouse and viewed from the west[84]

In October 1837 the following notice appeared in the Staffordshire Advertiser:-

On Sunday Morning, the 29th instant, The Solemn Service of HIGH MASS will be celebrated in the Catholic Chapel of Tixall, and a SERMON will be preached by the Hon. & Rev. GEORGE SPENCER At the Vespers Service in the afternoon a Sermon will be preached by the Ven.& Right.Rev. the Lord Bishop of Cambysopolis and (in England) Vicar Apostolic of the Midland District. The morning service will commence at eleven o'clock and the afternoon at half-past three.[85]

The Rev. Thomas Laurance Green was born in Stourbridge in 1799, the son of Francis Green of Solihull Lodge and Stourbridge. He was educated at Sedgley Park, and at Oscott College, 15th August 1813.

Prior to his appointment at Tixall, he was at Norwich, where he published in 1830 a series of discourses on the principal controverted points of Catholic Doctrine lately delivered at the Catholic Chapel, St John's Market, Norwich.[58]

The Chapel at Tixall by J.Buckler 1841[86]
(Viewed from the south-west
with the side entrance to the Hall behind)

The Chapel at Tixall 1841 by J.Buckler [87]
(Viewed from the south-east just behind the Gatehouse)

This may explain his enthusiasm for publishing his correspondence with the Rev.William Webb concerning the burial of Roman Catholics at Tixall.[61]

He left Tixall in 1845, and was Chaplain at St Mary's Priory, Princethorpe, Rugby from 1848 until 1858. He was the last of a long line of Catholic Chaplains at Tixall:-

CATHOLIC CHAPLINS AT TIXALL

Year	Name	Years	Ref
c1640			
c1678	Mr Evers		3
?	Rev Wilson		88
?	Rev. Chr Layfield		88
1756	George Beeston	35	88
1791	Michael Pembridge	?	88
1798	Thomas Price	12	89
1810	Henry Le Sage	11	89
1821	Robert Richmond	9	89
1830	Thomas L.Green	14	83,89

In 1833 the Sir Thomas Clifford, who had inherited estates at Burton Constable in Yorkshire, moved there and put his Tixall and Haywood Estates up for sale.

The sale particulars refer to:-
"THE VENERABLE GATEHOUSE OF TIXALL
through which is approached
THE BEAUTIFUL STONE CHAPEL"

The Estates were eventually bought by the Earl of Shrewsbury, living at Ingestre, in 1845.

An acre of land at Great Haywood was reserved from the sale and was given, along with the 1828 Catholic Chapel, to the local catholics who arranged for it to be moved there in 1845.

The marks made to facilitate re-building, are still present on the stonework inside.

Pevsner describes it as follows in 1974:-[90]

" Very much the character of an ambitious private chapel.
Ornate W front with a recessed high octagonal SW turret.
Along the sides large transomed Late Perpendicular windows,
all straight-headed.
Inside the dado below them is all stone-panelled.
Rich WEST GALLERY.
The new ceiling is a pity."

Clifford Arms from above
entrance in porch at RC Church
in Great Haywood

9. The 1848 Church at Tixall

When the Archdeacon visited Tixall Church on October 12th 1841, he reported as follows:-[76]

"Directions to the Churchwardens:-
(1) The state of the Fabric to be examined by a competent Surveyor, with reference, more especially, to the cracks in the North and South walls of the Chancel; and his opinion reported to the Archdeacon.
(2) The outer door at the West end of the Church to be well oiled with boiled linseed oil, and a new weatherboard put to the bottom of it: the inner door to be painted.
(3) The Communion Table, and oak pewing, to be well rubbed with boiled linseed oil.
(4) The coping stones, at each end of the roof, to be well pointed.
(5) The open drain round the Church to be kept clear from weeds and herbage.
(6) The Churchyard gate to be repaired and painted.

N.B. It would on many accounts be extremely desirable to take down the body of the Church, and rebuild it. Should this be done, the above directions will, of course , be superseded. I have written to Mr Marsland on this subject."

As we have already noted with respect to the Catholic Chapel, at this time the Tixall Estates were in the process of being purchased by the 2nd Earl Talbot of Ingestre.

The sale particulars included:-

"THE ADVOWSON OF THE CHURCH AND PARSONAGE HOUSE OF TIXALL
(Subject to the Life of the present Incumbent)"

Earl Talbot's third son, John Chetwynd Talbot, then decided to have Tixall Church rebuilt at his expense as an act of piety and so that it could be his mausoleum.

The following account appeared in 1849:-[65]

"The old church, which consisted of a nave, of which the architectural details had been destroyed by natural decay, a tower of very debased character, and a chancel of comparatively recent date, was taken down in consequence of the dilapidated state of the building generally, and the accommodation being insufficient to meet the needs of the parish, and to make way for a more suitable and ecclesiastical structure."

The new Church was consecrated on Whit-Tuesday 1849:-[91]

Tixall Church and Churchyard
Sentence of Consecration

In the name of God Amen Whereas it hath been represented unto us the Right Reverend Father in God John by Divine permission Lord Bishop of Lichfield by and on behalf of the Right Honorable Henry John Earl Talbot of Ingestrie in the County of Stafford and within our Diocese of Lichfield the Reverend William Webb Clerk Master of Arts the Rector and James Tyrer Esquire the Church Warden of the Parish of Tixall aforesaid and of several others Parishioners and Inhabitants of the said Parish that the Parish Church of Tixall was very ancient and by length of time had become very ruinous and dilapidated

and that the same had been recently taken down and a new Church erected and built over the site of the ancient one but upon an extended scale with a Pulpit Reading desk pews seats and sitting places therein at the sole cost and expense of the Honorable John Chetwynd Talbot of New Court Temple London one of Her Majestys Counsel learned on the law containing whithin the walls thereof fifty seven feet in length and sixteen feet in breadth the North Aisle being twenty eight feet long and eight feet and a half wide

and that the same hath been furnished with a Communion Table and Rails a font for baptizing Children a Bell and all things requisite and necessary for a Church and that twenty six pews have been erected therein containing ninety six sittings and four Benches containing twenty four sittings for Children

And Whereas it hath been further represented unto Us that the Land formerly used as a back way or road to the Rectory House of Tixall aforesaid hath been stopped up and added to the Church Yard of Tixall aforesaid and a new Road in lieu thereof hath been made out of Land belonging to the said Right Honorable Henry John Earl Talbot and which is more particularly described in the map or plan drawn in the margin of these presents and therein coloured Blue

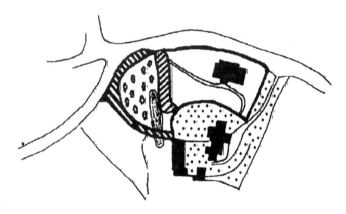

PLAN OF TIXALL CHURCHYARD

Present Ch. Yard -   ▬

Proposed Additions -   //////

New Backroad to Parsonage -   ◤◤◤◤

Grounds belonging to Parsonage -   ⟨ . . . ⟩

and which said land so as aforesaid added to the said Church Yard and intended to be consecrated as an additional burial Ground thereto contains in the whole about Two hundred square yards being Glebe Land and lies on the West side of the Church Yard of the said Parish of Tixall and hath been laid to and enclosed with the said Church Yard by a substantial fence and that the said newly erected Church and the Land so as aforesaid enclosed are ready for Consecration

And Whereas we have been duly petitioned to dedicate and consecrate the said newly erected Church by the name of "Saint John the Baptist" (by which name the ancient Church was dedicated) for the public Worship of Almighty God therein as and for the Parish Church of the Parish of Tixall aforesaid in lieu and substitution of the said ancient Church lately taken down and to decree that the same may be severed and so indeed to sever it from all common profane and secular uses and by the word of God and prayers and other Spiritual Benedictions and religious duties to dedicate and consecrate the same and all thereunto belonging to the sacred and ever Blessed name of God and to his Service and Worship

And also to consecrate the aforesaid Land laid to and enclosed with the said ancient Church Yard as a Cemetery or Burial Ground in addition to the said ancient Church Yard and to decree the same to be severed from all common profane and secular uses and to be consecrated Ground accordingly

Therefore We John by Divine permission Lord Bishop of Lichfield by virtue of our Episcopal authority Do set apart and separate the said newly erected Church at Tixall wherein We now are from all common profane and secular uses whatsoever and do consecrate and dedicate the same by the name of "Saint John the Baptist" to the Glory and for the worship of Almighty God and the celebration of Divine Offices and for the solemnization of marriages therein according to the rules and ceremonies of the United Church of England and Ireland as by Law established and for preaching and expounding the word of God therein for ever as and for the Parish Church of Tixall aforesaid in lieu and substitution of the said ancient Parish Church

And We do pronounce decree and declare by these presents that the said newly erected Church hath been and is so consecrated by Us and for the Parish Church of the Parish of Tixall aforesaid in lieu of the said ancient Parish Church and ought forever so to remain

And We do also set apart the aforesaid Land laid to and enclosed with the said ancient Church Yard from all common profane and secular uses whatsoever and do consecrate the same wholly and only as and for a Cemetery or Burial Ground in addition to the said Church Yard of the said Parish of Tixall for ever hereafter

And We do by these presents pronounce decree and declare that the same is so consecrated by Us and ought for ever so to remain

Lastly We reserve to the Archbishop of Canterbury and his Successors to Us and our Successors Bishops of Lichfield Our Chancellor and Official and to the Archdeacon of Stafford and their Successors a power of visiting the said Church and Church Yard in the same manner as other Churches and Churchyards within our Diocese are usually visited

and of exercising all Ecclesiastical Jurisdiction right power and authority in and over the same and the Incumbent and Officers thereof from time to time for ever hereafter

In Testimony whereof we have caused our Episcopal Seal to be hereunto affixed and have subscribed our name hereto this twenty ninth day of May in the year of our Lord One thousand eight hundred and forty nine and in the sixth year of our Consecration.

Signed Sealed and delivered by the within named John Lord Bishop of Lichfield (being first duly stamped) in the presence of

H.E.Coldwell MA Rector of Stafford and Rural Dean
Francis F Blackburne Incumbent of Cannock
J.Mott NP D^n Reg^r

According to the report in the Staffordshire Advertiser, on Whit Tuesday May 29th 1949,[65] the "day was delightfully fine", and the Church was crowded to excess, "and some indeed were unable to obtain admittance."

At 11am the Bishop was met at the Church Porch by the registrar of the diocese. After the initial formalities, the Bishop and Clergy processed in repeating alternately the 24th Psalm.

The Rev.William Webb read Morning Prayer, the Lessons were read by the Hon. & Rev. A.C.Talbot, and the Communion Service was read by the Bishop assisted by the Rev.W.E.Coldwell, Rector of St Mary's,Stafford and Rural Dean.

The sermon was preached by the Rev.Dr.Hook, Vicar of Leeds, probably a friend of John Chetwynd Talbot's, as he subsequently came to his funeral at Tixall.[92]

The text was from Corinthians I chapter 3 verses 16 & 17:-

"Know ye not that ye are the temple of God, and that the spirit of God dwelleth in you ?

If any man defile the temple of God, him shall God destroy, for the temple of God is holy, which temple ye are."

"The sermon was a masterly production, justifying the high reputation of the preacher as a profound theologian, and a consummate elocutionist.

Many who heard it pronounced it to be the perfection of pulpit oratory.

There was almost an entire absence of any peculiarities of sentiment likely to prove distasteful to any class of hearers, and the discourse was listened to throughout with the most fixed attention, and with great apparent edification, satisfaction and delight."[65]

The collection was towards the cost of erecting schools at Hixon, and raised £62.

Those attending the service included:-
Earl Talbot; The Hon & Mrs J.C.Talbot; The Hon & Rev.ACT Talbot; The Hon. Wellington Talbot; The Hon.& Mrs Gerald Talbot; The Hon. & Rev.H.Bagot; The Rev.W.E.Coldwell and many other local clergy; J.Bramley Moore,Esq. Mayor of Liverpool (no doubt at the invitation of James Tyrer); James Tyrer,Esq.; R.B.Levett,Esq.; W.D.Webb,Esq. of Haselour; Harvey Wyatt,Esq.; E.D.Moore,Esq.; Charles Turner, Esq.(Great grandson of the Rev.Ralph Turner of Tixall); J.T.Harland, Esq., MD.; and Mr Brandon, the architect.

Immediately after the consecration of the Church, the Bishop and 35 clergy consecrated the recent addition to the Churchyard, land that had previously served as the back entrance to the Rectory.

The Bishop and other important guests, a party of about 70, were then invited by Mr Tyrer to Tixall Hall where they partook of a splendid cold collation.

Meanwhile, the Rev.William Webb entertained a party of about 30 at the Rectory.

The Church was erected from designs of Wyatt and Brandon, under the superintendence of Mr Brandon, " and the beautiful little structure does credit to the taste of these gentlemen."[65]

This is confirmed in the description for Grade B Listing,[93] which says that the Church is:-

"notable as having a little altered Victorian interior and as being a careful interpretation of the Early English style and a good example of the work of T.H.Wyatt and David Brandon, architects of London."

The encaustic floor tiles are by Minton, and were the gift of James Tyrer, Esq.

They include an interesting motive at the nave crossing, which according to Arthur Poole[94] (Rector 1955 -1980) commemorates the Consecration of the new Church in 1849:-

The Date: MDCCCXLIX, ie. AD 1849.......... ①
John Chetwynd Talbot: JCT .... ②
James Tyrer, Churchwarden: JT ...... ③
William Webb, Rector: WW.......... ④
2nd Earl Talbot: T & Peers Coronet.......... ⑤
Victoria Regina: VR Crowned .... ⑥

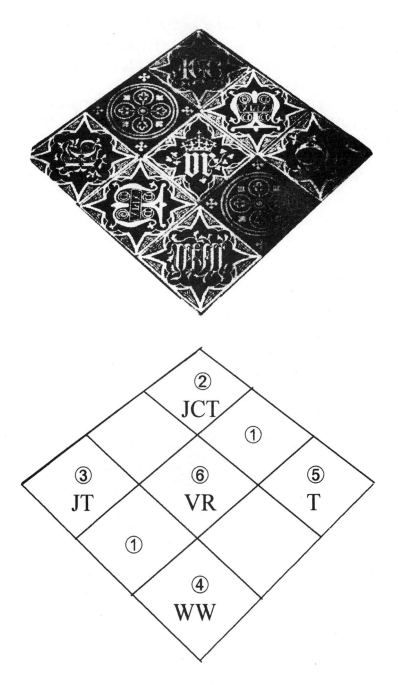

The church is built of keuper sandstone, most probably from the nearby Tixall quarries. The roof is of Staffordshire Blue Tiles.

The stone was given by the late Earl Talbot, " and was carried to the spot by his Lordship's principal tenants residing in the parish."[65]

The records for Salt Quarries, which were the stone quarries owned by Earl Talbot at Weston and Tixall, show stone for Tixall Church in 1848 and 1849.[95]

The building work was executed by Mr Ward of Brocton, and Mr Chatfield, builder of Stafford.[65]

According to White[96] the Parish Church was "rebuilt in 1849 in the style of the old one and is a small neat fabric with stained glass windows."

However the 1848 Church is very different from the 1782 Church both in ground-plan and general style:-

The entrance is now via a porch on the south of the Nave, and a north aisle has been added to increase the seating capacity.

Carved heads on either side of the entrance porch

The carved heads may be Victorian representations of St Chad, who was appointed bishop of the Mercians in 669, and thus was the first Bishop of Lichfield; and Ethelfleda, widow of Ethelred the ealdorman of Mercia, who fortified Stafford and Tamworth, and died at Tamworth in 918. St Chad had died of the plague in 672.[97]

Pevsner describes the church as:-[90]
"Nave with bellcote and chancel.
Low N aisle.
Small windows with pointed-trefoiled heads."

The Western open Bellcote houses a single bell 19" diameter and 1½cwts, Note A, with a wrought steel headstock and lever with a chain.

The present bell was recast by John Taylor of Loughborough in 1960 at a cost of £43. 12s 6d including £1. 12s. 6d for the returnable packing case.[98]

The previous bell was described as "not a good casting - numerous blow holes, poor tone, and too large." and was inscribed:-
"C. et G.Mears Londini fecerunt   Gloria in excelsis Deo MDCCCXLIII" or
" C & G Mears of London made it Glory be to God on High 1843"

The ground-plan of the new church shows the layout with 4 benches for the children to the north of the pulpit and possibly some kind of heating stove or boiler in the corner of the vestry[68]:-

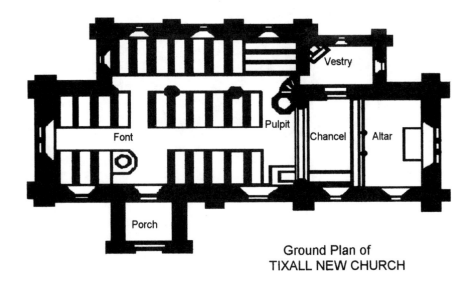

Ground Plan of
TIXALL NEW CHURCH

The area to the north of the pulpit was modified to make a new boiler room when central heating was installed in 1979.

John Chetwynd Talbot died at Brighton on Tuesday evening May 26th, 1852,[99] aged 45, having lived in the City of Westminster.
On the previous Friday, he had been:-
"engaged in active prosecution of his professional duties, but, it is feared, that a too energetic application to them superinduced the sudden death.
Cause of death is ascribed to water on the chest."[99] *(Heart Failure)*

On Whit Tuesday 1852 his mortal remains " found an appropriate resting place in a vault, which on the re-building of the

Church, he had caused to be constructed underneath the Chancel.."[100]

The body of the deceased was brought to Colwich Station on the morning of the internment and was conveyed in the hearse to Tixall Hall, from which the funeral cortege, unostentatious and simple in all its appointments, proceeded to the neighbouring Church."[99]

Those present included:-The widow and her two sons; a large party of Talbot relations; Rev.Dr Hook, Vicar of Leeds; Thos. Hartshorne,Esq.*(Resident at Brancote)*; Thos.Salt Esq.; and R.W.Hand,Esq.*(Solicitor ?)*

"The service was impressively read by the Rev.W.Webb, Rector of Tixall" with the help of three other Clergy.

A bronze plaque on the right of the sanctuary records:-
The Parish Church of St John the Baptist, Tixall
was reconsecrated on Whit Tuesday 1849
It was entirely rebuilt at the sole charge of
the Hon.[ble] John Chetwynd Talbot whose mortal remains were
deposited in a vault underneath the Chancel on Whit Tuesday 1852
All the sittings are free.
William Webb MA Rector
James Tyrer church Warden

A bronze plaque in a Stone Niche on left of the Sanctuary has the inscription:-
In Memory of the Hon John Chetwynd Talbot
third son of Charles Chetwynd second Earl Talbot,
Queens Council, Attorney General to H.R.H. the Prince of Wales,
Deputy High Steward of the University of Oxford
Born May XXXI MDCCCVI
Died May XXVI MDCCCLII
Into thy hands I commend my Spirit:
for thou hast redeemed me, O LORD thou GOD of truth.

An adjacent plaque records his wife:-

In Memory of the Hon Caroline Jane Chetwynd Talbot
widow of the Hon John Chetwynd Talbot
and daughter of the 1st Baron Wharncliffe
Born June 13th 1809
Died June 12th 1876
One generation shall raise Thy Works unto another

In 1871 the following account appeared,[100]:-
"The readers of the Trent Valley Magazine will bear with the
compiler of the Annals of Tixall in paying a passing tribute to the
virtues of the re-builder of its Parish Church.

Admirable as a son, husband, parent, brother, friend, and master,
Mr Talbot was distinguished as an advocate by uprightness and
honesty of purpose, which, combined with his irreproachable
character, contributed even more than his undoubted talents and
industry to place him in the foremost rank of the profession he
adorned.

A sincere and conscientious Christian gentleman, his was not the
mere form of godliness, — the presence of its power was manifested
by its fruits.

He was a true-hearted son, if ever there was one, of the Church to
which it is our happiness to belong, — thoroughly appreciating its
privileges, and ardently desirous to promote its extension and
efficiency.

The records of our Church societies testify to his having been one
of their most active and liberal supporters from the commencement
of his professional career.

How he loved the House of God, and the place where His honour
dwelleth, not Tixall alone bears witness, but many others also, to
which he was a large and cheerful contributor.

At the time of his death he was erecting, at his sole cost, another
temple to God's honour and worship, in the locality he had fixed
upon for his own residence.

Thus did he on principle dedicate to the Lord the first-fruits of his professional gains.

His was no ostentatious Churchmanship, taken up, as some will say of themselves, as though they did the Church honour by espousing her cause.

No one could have witnessed his reverent demeanour in the House of God, and the deep devotional tone of his responses, without being fully persuaded that piety and religious feeling were there, and that his Churchmanship and his religion were something more than a mere name—that they were a reality."

Unfortunately when his widow died in 1876 a few years after this account was written, she left instructions that she and husband were both to be buried at Markbeech in Kent.

This is recorded in a plaque on the right side of the Sanctuary:-

The body of the Hon.[ble] J.C.Talbot founder of this Church
was removed to Markbeech Church, Kent & laid there by the side of
his Widow according to her desire. July 8.1876.
In their death they were not divided.

Hence like Ralph Turner and Simon Wakelin before him, John Chetwynd Talbot was destined not to remain undisturbed with his memorial in the Chancel of Tixall Church.

The burials of Ralph and Simon having no doubt been disturbed during the previous two re-buildings, and Simon Wakelin's memorial re-located during the 1849 re-building.

John Chetwynd Talbot is also commemorated by a very fine window by Willement on the North side of the Chancel at Ingestre:-

" To the Glory of God and to the beloved memory of the Hon.
John Chetwynd Talbot son of the 2nd Earl Talbot who died 26th of
May 1852 this window is dedicated by his son."

Possibly this additional memorial was felt necessary when John Chetwynd Talbot's remains had been removed to Kent against his wishes.

The stained glass windows in the Chancel at Tixall are by Bennett & Son of York. All the windows were restored in 1992.

The East window shows scenes from the life of St John, and was presented to the Church by the Rector, the Rev. William Webb.[65]

The smaller windows on the south side of the Chancel show a Priest of 1849 at Holy Communion and at Baptism.

The south window nearest the east end with the Priest at Holy Communion, was donated by Charles Turner, Esq. of Liverpool, the great grandson of Ralph Turner,[65] *(See pages 37 - 38)* and has the inscription:

"To the Glory of God and memory of the
Reverend Ralph Turner
Rector of this Parish AD MDCCLX Aged XLV"

S.Chancel window
to Ralph Turner

The West Nave window is in memory of the two young wives of George Woodward, who both died at Tixall Hall in childbirth.

It has the following inscriptions:-

" TRUST IN THE LORD AND WAIT PATIENTLY FOR HIM"

" BLESSED ARE THE PURE IN HEART FOR THEY SHALL SEE GOD"

"BLESSED ARE THE MERCIFUL FOR THEY SHALL OBTAIN MERCY"

"TO THE MEMORY OF ANNE DEAVILLE WIFE OF G.R.WOODWARD
DIED 1851 AGED 30"

"TO THE MEMORY OF ANNE JANE WIFE OF G.R.WOODWARD
DIED 1845 AGED 28"

They were related to James Tyrer, who lived at Tixall Hall and was Church Warden at the time the Church was rebuilt in 1848.

James Tyrer was born at Formby, nr.Liverpool, and appears to have been a batchelor.

In 1841 he was living at Linacre Grove, Marsh Lane, Bootle, Liverpool with two servants.
In 1842 he took up residence at Tixall Hall renting the Hall from Sir Clifford Constable,[101] and in 1845 he was paying the Earl of Shrewsbury £390pa for the rent of the Hall and grounds; 5 cottages; Fishing in the River Sow from Haywood to Brancote; Hunting, Hawking, Shooting and Coursing over the Estate Farms; and Shooting at St Thomas; (Hares on the Brancote Farms were reserved for the tenants)[102]

In the 1851 Census he was described as a Merchant Ship Owner, aged 53, and was living with his widowed sister in law Sarah, his young nephew William Woodward, aged 9,niece Annie Woodward, aged 8, their Swiss Governess, a housekeeper, butler, page, cook, 2 housemaids, 2 houseservants, and a chairwoman.
His coachman, with wife and 4 children were living in the Stableyard.

He was chief of one of the oldest established shipping firms of Liverpool, based at a house in the Old Churchyard.[101] (*Presumably by St Nicholas's Church near the Pierhead*) He:-
"did not readily fall into the modern ways and he did not carry on

business in palatial offices, but the house was none the less respected for its antiquity."

He was one of the first to send ships and open up the English trade on the west coast of South America.

He was one of the oldest members of Liverpool Municipal Council, having been elected without a contest for the Exchange Ward in 1844, "in the Conservative interest."[101]

In 1868 he was elected Alderman for the Great George Ward, and he retained that position until his death.

He was a JP for Stafford Borough, and was also on the commission for peace for Staffordshire.

Hence in the 1871 census James Tyrer was described as a Magistrate, Alderman and Ship-owner.

The following year, 1872, he moved to Bournemouth where he died three years later in 1875 aged 82.

George Ratcliffe Woodward or his first wife, were James's nephew or niece. George was a merchant and lived at Tixall Hall. His first wife, Anne Jane died on April 15th 1845.

Their son, William Ratcliffe, mentioned in the 1851 census, died on April 21st, 1855, aged 13 at Tixall. He was known as Trappie.[103]

Annie, Williams sister, continued to live with her uncle.

She married Hopton Scott Stewart, a Captain in the 11th Regiment on April 24th 1867 at Tixall Church. In the marriage register, Hopton's father was described as late colonial secretary of Jamaica.

On March 2nd 1848 George Ratcliffe, widower, married Anne Deaville Owen.

She died on December 26th 1851, aged 30, 5 days after the baptism of her third child, Sarah Helen Anne at Tixall. Sarah Helen had been born on December 11th.

According to the 1861 census, Sarah Helen, aged 9, was still living at Tixall Hall with her brothers, George Ratcliffe, aged 12 and and Basil Hall, aged 11. Both brothers were christened at St Nicholas', Liverpool.

George Ratcliffe married for a third time, Eliza Sophie Bland from Hindworth, Warwicks, at St John's Church, Preston on October 11th, 1856, but had no further children.

The grave of James Tyrer and his relatives in Tixall Churchyard

10. Other Churches with Tixall Associations

Tixall has connections with at least two other churches:
St Thomas's, Castletown, Stafford,
and St Oswald's, Lower Peover.

St Thomas's Church at Castletown was built in 1866 and demolished in 1972, when the parish church was moved to Doxey[104,105,106]

In 1861 the area by the railway station at Castletown had a population of about 800 with no church or school.

Even by 1866 the streets had not been made up and there was little provision for drainage.

The terraced houses mainly had 2 rooms upstairs and 2 rooms downstairs with a scullery downstairs and a lavatory across the yard.

There were some larger 3 bedroomed houses with a pigsty in the backgarden, and some houses had 2 cellar rooms; one for coal and/or wood, and one for use as a workshop if required.

The average household consisted of 6, with the men working on the railway in shifts.

"It was common practice for engine drivers and firemen to go straight from work to one of the several local pubs, for example the "Sir Robert Peel" conveniently situated close to the railway station and the workmen's homes.

There they would sit drinking until their wives ran upwith their hot dinners between two plates.

They would carry on drinking as they ate, and then go straight off to their next shift."[107,]

Obviously there were no Health & Safety at Work Regulations at that time.

In 1860 a subscription list was opened to provide a church and school for the area.

By 1862 a total of £458 - 1s - 6d had been raised, including donations of £200 from Edward Lyon Esq., and £100 from the LNWR.[105]

Land was bought from Lord Stafford for £50, and in 1863 a plain, cheap schoolroom for 150 children was built at a cost of £295 - 14s - 7d. Initially the schoolroom was used for occasional services.

The committee proposed to use the remaining £162 - 16s - 11d to build a church with a permanent chancel and a temporary nave of iron or wood at an estimated cost of at least £600.

However adequate financial support was not forthcoming until James Tyrer of Tixall, a major railway shareholder,

"who had the welfare of railway workers and the town of Stafford at heart, offered to build and endow the church entirely at his own cost."[107]

The Church was intended mainly for the railway workers living in the area, and all the sittings were free.

It was to be a distinct incumbency from St Paul's Parish, and was styled as a vicarage from 1868 when the boundaries were finalised.

The church was designed by W.Culshaw of Liverpool in a mixed Early English and Decorated style.[105]

It was built by F.Ratcliffe of Stafford, using stone from Grinshill, nr. Shrewsbury and walling from

St Thomas's, Castletown[108]   Staffs.Newsl.

-93-

Burnsley in Lancs. which was carried over the LNWR track free of charge.

The nave was 75'6" x 28'6" and the chancel 28' x 20'. It was designed to seat 500.[105]

The floor tiles, eg. around the font, appear to be similar to those at Tixall, and were probably also by Minton.

These tiles were a favourite with Victorian Church builders.

There was a square organ chamber (housing the excellent organ by John Banfield of Birmingham) and an octagonal vestry, on either side of the chancel.

"The seats were divided into side and central compartments by side aisles, there being no central aisle, which is regarded as an important feature where processions occupy a prominent place in the services."[105]

Font showing floor tiles[107]

The bell was made by John Rudhall of Gloucester and dated 1799. It is not known where it had come from.

A parsonage, also designed by W.Culshaw was built by Adams & Pemberton of Stafford, on an acre of land by the road leading to

Rowley Hall, which later became Rowley Avenue. The grounds being "tastefully laid out" by Mr Sandy.[105]

The Church, Parsonage, Endowment of the Living, and Repair Fund, cost Tyrer £11,000:-

Total cost of Church and Fittings   £3000

Parsonage and grounds   £2000

Living endowed   £200 pa

(more when the Ecclesiastical Commissioners raise this to £300)

Fund to give £5/yr for repairs

More information on these endowments is given in the Consecration Document:-[109]

In the Name of God Amen. Whereas it hath been represented unto us The Right Reverend Father in God John by Divine permission Lord Bishop of Lichfield by and on the part and behalf of

the Reverend Nevill George Murray Lawrence Clerk Incumbent or Minister of the perpetual Curacy and parish Church of Forebridge in the parish of Castlechurch in the County of Stafford and within our Diocese of Lichfield

James Tyrer of Tixall in the said County of Stafford Esquire and John Morgan and Edward Mousley Churchwardens of the District or Parish of Forebridge aforesaid and of several parishioners and inhabitants of the said Parish

that the District parish of Forebridge aforesaid is become very populous and in order to promote the interests of Religion and to provide Church Accommodation and aid for the Spiritual Wants of the Inhabitants of the said District

a Church or Chapel hath been erected there on the piece or parcel of land hereinafter mentioned capable of accommodating five hundred persons

the expenses of erecting and fitting up the same being about two thousand one hundred pounds and which have been entirely defrayed by the said James Tyrer Esquire

and that under and by virtue of a certain Deed of Conveyance bearing the date the seventh day of January one thousand eight hundred and sixty six the said James Tyrer under the Authority and for the purposes of certain Acts of Parliament therein recited Did thereby freely and voluntarily and without any valuable consideration

grant convey and release to Us as The Lord Bishop of Lichfield and to our heirs All that piece or parcel of land or ground containing by admeasurement two thousand four hundred and twenty square yards situate lying and being in Castletown in the parish of Castlechurch in the County of Stafford

which said piece of land is bounded on all sides by land belonging to Lord Stafford and the same is particularly delineatedon the plan drawn on the said presents and thereon coloured "Pink"

and all his Estate right tithe and interest of in and to the same land and hereditaments and every part thereof

To hold the same pieces of land untolls(?) the said John Lord Bishop of Lichfield and Our heirs To the Us the said John Lord Bishop of Lichfield and his successors for ever

for the purpose and to the intent that the same may for ever hereafter be set apart devoted used and dedicated as a site for the erecion of a new church

to be used and devoted when consecrated to the Service of Almighty God as a place of Divine Worship according to the Liturgy and usages of the united Church of England and Ireland and by law required in accordance with the above mentioned Act and all other statutory modifications thereof

And further representing unto Us that the said Church or Chapel erected on part of the said piece or parcel of land or ground tinted "Pink" on the said plan contains within the Walls thereof seventy five feet six inches in length and thirty six feet six incehs in width

And that the same Church has been furnished with a Communion Table and Rails and with the necessary Plate for the Communion of the Holy Sacrament a Pulpit reading Desk Seats and sitting places a Font for baptizing Children a Bell and all things necessary for a Church or Chapeland the same is ready for Consecration

And further representing unto Us that a sufficient sum by way of Endowment of the said Church or Chapel has been provided by the said James Tyrer having transferred unto the Honorable Dudley Francis Stuart Ryder commonly called Viscount Sandon

Thomas Berry Horsfall of Bellamour Hall near Rugeley in the County of Stafford Esquire M.P.

The Reverend Joseph Bardsley the Secretary home Mission London

John Campbell of the Grove Aigburth Liverpool Esquire

and Charles Walker Lyon of Silver Hill Barton under Needwood in the said County of Stafford Esquire

one thousand five hundred and twenty nine pounds stock in the Birkenhead

Railway Company
the sum of one thousand four hundred and sixty one pounds Guaranteed stock in the Great Western Railway Company
and fifty shares in the Kendal and Windermere Railway Company
And that under and by virtue of an Agreement bearing date the first day of June one thousand eight hundred and sixty five the patronage of the said sum .....? be ever hereafter to be vested in and exercised by the said James Tyrer his heirs and assigns
And further representing Us that twelve sittings are to be set apart for the Minister for the time being and his Family
and eight sittings for the use of the churchwardens
and that the remainder of the sittings are to be set apart as free sittings for the use of the Inhabitants of the District of CastleTown aforesaid to resort thereto to hear Divine Service therein

And Whereas we have been duly petitioned to dedicate and consecrate the said Church or Chapel by the name of "Saint Thomas" for the public worship of Almighty God therein
and to decree that the same may be severed and so indeed to sever it from all common profane and secular uses whatsoever
and by the word of God and prayers and other spiritual Benedictions and Religious Duties to dedicate and consecrate the same and all thereunto belonging to the sacred and ever blessed Name of God and to his Service and worship
and to be used as a Church or Chapel for the performance of Divine Service and Offices therein according to the rites and ceremonies of the United Church of England and Ireland as by law established
and for preaching and expounding the Word of God therein for ever hereafter
And We do by these presents pronounce decree and declare that the same hath been and is so consecrated by us and ought forever so to remain
And we hereby reserve and saving always the right and interest of the said District Church of Forebridge and the Incumbent and Offices thereof in all and singular the rights fees privileges profits and emoluments whatsoever to the same and to them by Law or Custom in any way belonging or appertaining
Lastly we reserve to the Archbishop of Canterbury and his successors to us and our successors Bishops of Lichfield our Chancellor and Official and to the Archdeacon of Stafford and their successors the right and juridisdiction

in and over the premises and a power of visiting the said Church or Chapel in the same manner and with the like authority as Churches within our Diocese are usually visited

All and singular which premises as far as in us lie we decree confirm and establish by these presents In witness whereof we have caused Our Episcopal Seal to be hereunto affixed and have subscribed Our name hereto this seventh day of May in the year of our Lord one thousand eight hundred and sixty six and in the twenty third year of our Consecration

The first incumbent was the Rev.Evan Kendall who had previously served 10 years at Kennilworth with the Rev.Bickmore.

The service of consecration was on Monday May 7th 1866 at 11.30am.

The advance notice[106] said that at the request of Mr Tyrer, there would be no collections at the services on May 7th, but:-

"Should, however, any one be disappointed at not having an opportunity of assisting in so good a work, we would venture to suggest that if a subscription were got up to purchase and remove the cottages which partially hide the view of the church from the Newport Road it would add the last finishing touch to the noble gift of Mr Tyrer."

"The attendance at the morning service was very numerous and comprised a large number of the nobility and gentry of the country .... long before the service commenced the church was crowded and the aisles were soon full to the very outside of the porch."[105]

The Bishop of Lichfield consecrated the church in the morning, his 147th consecration while in office.

The morning sermon was preached by the Rev.Hugh McNeile,DD, Canon of Chester, had been a friend of Mr Tyers for 40 years:

"It was an extempore discourse, the rev. doctor having nothing in his hand but a small Bible, from which he read the text which was taken from part of the 22nd and 23rd verses of the 16th chapter of St John's Gospel."[105]

After the morning service "A very choice collation" was prepared by Mrs Fraser in the Railway Station Dining-room.

Mr Tyrer, who had invited a very distinguished company, presided.

There were speeches and toasts by James Tyrer; the Bishop; the Lord Lieutenant; the Rev.N.G.M.Lawrence of St Pauls; and Mr Groves, Treasurer of the Church Building Society in Liverpool.

The Earl of Shrewsbury and Talbot toasted the Ladies - Lady Lichfield and Miss Woodward, James Tyrer's great-niece.

There were then further speeches and toasts from the Ven.Archdeacon Moore; the Rev.Bickmore, Vicar of Kenilworth; and the Rev.W.Kendall of St Thomas's.

The Rev.James Bardsley MA, Rector of St Ann's Manchester, preached at the Evening Service.

The people of Castletown showed their gratitude by subsequently presenting James Tyrer with an oak reading desk, a bible, a book of common prayer, a family prayer book, and a copy of the hymn book to be used at St Thomas's Church.

The front of the reading desk was covered with needlework in the centre of which was worked Mr Tyrer's monogram, and round the border were the words:-

"Presented to James Tyrer,Esq. by the congregation of St Thomas's Church, Castletown, AD 1866."

The presentation was made at Tixall Hall in the presence of

some of Mr Tyrers neighbours including Mr T.B.Horsfall MP and the Rev.W.Webb, with a testimonial and an address "beautifully engrossed and bound in morocco".[107]

Problems subsequently arose because the Rev Kendall was such a good preacher:-

"We hear loud complaints that this church which has been built and the parsonage also with its endowment of £200 a year, by the munifence of Mr James Tyrer at a cost of £11,000, is not appropriated to the wishes of its founder as it should be.

The church is frequented by persons going out of the town, who neglect their own parish churches to occupy space in a building which was never designed for them, something like the cuckoos that wait till the sparrows have built their nests and then occupy them.

The church was intended for the working classes attached to the railway in particular and intended to be free to their use.

Fine silks and satins with extensive crinolines are a bar to the working classes in more ways than one.

We understand that the clergyman is an excellent preacher and conducts the services in harmony with the tastes of the Evangelicals. The church is so full of an evening that unless you go a quarter of an hour before time, you can not get a seat."[110]

James Tyrer died at Hume Tower, in Bournemouth on June 20th 1875 at quarter to one on Sunday morning.

He had spent the winter in Bournemouth with his great-nephew Capt.Hopton Stewart, who was also staying there for the benefit of his health.

On Monday evening there was a most impressive religious service in the drawing room at Hume Tower, when the family and servants partook of Holy Communion.

"On Tuesday, the deceased remains enclosed in a shell, a lead coffin, and an outer coffin of polished oak with silver fittings were brought by train to Stafford and thence conveyed to Tixall, where they were deposited in the library at the Hall on a table draped in black, and surrounded by a choice collection of greenhouse plants."

The remains of the deceased gentleman were interred on Thursday in the family vault at the rear of Tixall Church, the arrangements for the funeral being of the most simple character.

The coffin was borne along the private walk from the Hall to the Church by eight servants and was preceded by the Rev.W.Webb, Rector of Tixall and the Rev W. Kendall, Vicar of St Thomas's Stafford; Mr E.F.Weston, family surgeon; Mr W.C.Woodroffe, Haywood Abbey; Mr Field, family solicitor; Mr Warren, butler; Mr P.Ridge, valet; Mr Jackson, gardener.

The mourners were:-

Capt.Hopton Stewart; Mr Ratcliffe Woodward; Mr Oliver Hatch and Mr James Laidlow, representing the Liverpool business establishment; Mr T.B.Horsfall of Bellamour.

Previous to the coffin being lowered into the vault, it was covered with devices of flowers by Capt Stewart, and before the vault was closed up, Mr Warren on behalf of the servants at Bournemouth, also laid flowers on and around the coffin.

The mournful ceremony was witnessed by a large number of villagers, many of whom shed tears as the concluding portions of the burial service were being read."[96]

Presumably Mr Ratcliffe Woodward was Annnie Deaville Owen's eldest son, who had been 9 in the 1861 census (page 91)

Subsequently, James Tyer's great-niece Mrs Walter Eaton, (Annie Woodward, Capt.Hopton Stewart's widow) presented the church of St Thomas's at Castletown with a memorial window made by Messrs Burleson & Grylls, with the inscription:-

Born on the Feast of the Annunciation 1793
Entered to rest June 20th 1875

The second Church is more tenuously connected with Tixall, being an unsigned oil painting on galvanized iron, found in the vestry around 1980:-

The base of galvanized iron suggests a date of after 1900.

The painting appears to be the work of an amateur artist showing St Oswald's Church, Lower Peover, nr Knutsford:-

The painting could be a gift to a Vicar retiring from St Oswald's, or to someone else with strong connections with Lower Peover.

However a list of St Oswald's vicars does not show any obvious link with known Tixall residents:-

VICARS OF ST OSWALD'S, LOWER PEOVER 1831 - 1959

1831	John Holme
1874	Thomas Harris
1877	Arthur Guest
1912	Hugh Henry Magrath Lefroy
1924	Thomas William Hunt
1940	Thomas Henry Pullen
1942	John Newman Ellwood
1949	Douglas Rene Tassell
1959	John Cyril Sladden

11. Tixall Church in the late 1800s & early 1900s

On May 30th, 1853, only 5 years after the Church was built, the Parochial Church Council Minutes include "the stained window in the South Wall of the Nave be attended to as to admit more light." [111]

Three years later on January 15th 1856 they include:-

"Church Rate of 2d/£1 to be forthwith levied for expenses incurred by the repairs of the roof of the North Aisle and other expenses of the Church during the current year."

Problems were also being experienced with the Church Heating as on Easter Monday, March 28th, 1864, the Minutes note: "Estimate for the more efficient warming of the Church to be procured." No doubt it had been a cold Easter Sunday !

It is interesting to note the Church Finances around this time. The Minutes for Easter Tuesday 1877 record:-

"37 offertories for church expenses from April 23 to March 25th

was £21 - 0s - 3½d

Expenses for year ending Easter 1877,   including £10 salary for

organist to Christmas 1876, was £24 - 1s - 6d

leaving a deficiency of £3 - 1s - 2½d which was made good out of the offertories at the disposal of the Rector"

Attendance at the Annual Meeting was not always good. On Easter Monday April 18th, 1881, the minutes record:-

"The Rector being present and the only parishioner putting in an appearance being Mr Mynors, and no other persons having been nominated for the office, the old churchwardens having previously expressed their willingness to serve were re-appointed accordingly."

Mr Mynors, was probably Mr Walter C.T.Mynors aged 42, who was then living at Brancote with his wife Martha, and farming 2,200 acres.

In January 1884, following the death of William Webb, Craven

Jervis Vincent was appointed Rector of Tixall. Presumably he was related to William P. Vincent, the Vicar of Salt.

Extensive repairs had been ordered to the Church and Rectory in June 1883 at an estimated cost of £54 - 10s 0d.[112]

These included:-

RECTORY;-

Painting and general repairs. Replace tiles and check guttering

Reinstate decayed ends of rafters of roof over Larder

Reinstate stone sill of front door

South elevation & adjoining outbuilding: Reinstate coping on ashpit wall, small ventilation window over garden closets, and back boarding of seat

Kitchen Yard: Take up and level all sunk paving. Reset coping stones to yard wall, reinstate top step to kitchen door, reinstate key to wash-house door, splice bottom of stickhouse door frame.

Cellar Staircase: Rebuild three brick steps.

Dining Room: Raise sunk end of hearthstone, fill up hole in cupboard

Study: fasten draught plate in hearthstone, ease door to garden

Kitchen Passage: Ease cellar and kitchen doors, quarries on floor

Kitchen: quarries on floor, ease cupboard door & door to larder, fasten mantle shelf, clean & repair cooking range and boiler

Dairy: Point under oak sill of salting trough & paving & plinth to same

Reference is also made to to the Cellars, Entrance Hall, Drawing Room, Pantry, and Larder.

Bedroom over Dining Room: Worm eaten floorboards

Back-landing & Bedroom over Kitchen: reinstate damaged part of plaster floor

Reference is also made to Bedrooms over the Hall, Drawing Room, and Larder, and to a Water Closet and Attics.

Wall between Churchyard and Garden: take down and rebuild, point stone wall round doorway and stone coping over same

Entrance Gate: take down and reset stone wall, clean and rub stone pillars

Furnace & Wall between Yard and Orchard: Furnace & Chimney, reset stone coping, fasten posts of wicket gate

Reference is also made to the stone wall at the bottom of the garden, and a sunk fence with wicket gate and iron fencing

Fowl Pens: brick, stone coping - cement up edging of tiles against walls, reinstate small lattice doors to fowl pens
Other Outbuildings included a Pigstye, Closet in orchard, Coalyard, Stables, Coachhouse, Barn, Saddle Room, Coachhouse, Two Stables, Barn and Lofts.

CHURCH:-
Clean moss and young trees off N.roof
Reinstate roof tiles, point open joints in ridge tiles, reinstate cement flashing and leave water-tight, the roof raining at both ends, point open joints of coping to gable, clean out and paint gutters and down trunks.

The repairs were apparently completed by February 22nd 1884.

In March 1884, the School Managers asked the Rector to advertise for a schoolmistress at £40 salary and 2/3 grant and fairly furnished house, and if she could play the harmonium in Church £10 extra. To be vetted by the Shrewsburys before appointed."[113]

At this time, from 1883 to 1905 Lord Shrewsbury was the Parishioners Churchwarden, with Henry Dodd and later George Stretton as Rectors Warden.(Appendix 1)

In 1887 the Rev.Craven J.Vincent was renting just over 13 acres from the Shrewsbury Estate at a rent of £40-1s a year.[114] This included the entrance drive to the Rectory & part of the front garden, and parts of Prestons Meadow, Great Meadow and Glebe Land.
In July 1988 he wrote " I regret I am unable to continue the land I at present hold from Lord Shrewsbury."
In June 1885, the 40 acres of glebelands (Part of Great Meadow, Ox Pasture, Great Ox Pasture, Pt of Salt Lodge, Coat Meadow, Coat Leasow & Part of Middle Field) were taken over by Lord Shrewsbury in exchange for 13 acres of land (orchards, drives,

etc.) adjacent to the Rectory, as part of a deal with the Land Office Inclosure Dept.

In September and October 1890, the Rev.Vincent published his own banns and must have married Gertrude Hopton of Upton Warren, Bromsgrove, soon after.

The 1891 entry for Tixall Rectory is unusual in that the wife is listed after the servants, instead of immediately after her husband:-

Craven J.Vincent	aged 35	Clerk	born Thurolaud, Yorks
Adlade Miles	aged 44	Domestic Servant	
Alber A.York	aged 15	Domestic Servant	
Gertrude Vincent	aged 22	Wife	born Bromsgrove
Annie Furnbank ?	aged 63	Aunt	born Leeds

Tixall School played an important part in the religious life of the village.

It had been moved to a new purpose built building in 1855 and on October 4th 1855 the site was conveyed by Lord Shrewsbury to the Rector and Churchwardens and their successors for ever:-[115]
" To permit and suffer the said piece of land together with the school room and buildings now built
to be used and appropriated for the education of poor children of both sexes of the said Parish of Tixall, without regard to the religious sentiments of their parents,
under the name and denomination of the Tixall School in the principles of the Established Church -
The said School and the affairs thereof to be under the management of a committee to consist of the Rector for the time being, and his curate (if any)
and the Churchwardens for the time being
and of two ladies or gentlemen being members of the Church of England to be annually chosen by the subscribers to the funds of the school."

As a Church School it was subject to annual inspections from the Diocese and in 1890, the inspector reported:-[116]

Report of Religious Instruction		Stds 5 - 2	1 & Inf
Knowledge of:-	Old Testament	Fair	V.Fair
	New Testament	Mod	Fair
	Catechism	Fair	Bad
	Prayer Book	Bad	Bad
Repetition of:-	Scripture	Good	Fair
	Hymns, Collects, etc.	Good	V.Fair
	Catechism	Good	V.Fair

The hope which I ventured to express in my last report has not, I regret to say, been realized.

After a careful examination I could come to no other conclusion than that the scriptural part of the work has been almost entirely neglected, as the children had aquired only the vaguest and most meagre knowledge of what was supposed to have been taught -

some of the subjects had not, as far as I could see been touched on.

The only thing that was at all satisfactory was the memory work and this was fairly well done in Division 1.

There was a significant improvement in the years following and in July 1897 a new teacher, Mr R.White was being appointed at a salary of £40 a year with half the Government Grant (Total £56 - 14s 6d) and a furnished house with coals.

The correspondence about his appointment included the following from the Rev. Vincent:-[117]

" As has been usual with all our teachers they have taken Sunday School each Sunday morning from 10 to 11, and one hours Choir practice a week.

I take it for granted that you will do the same. We have a paid Organist for the Church Services."

Mr White replied that he was quite willing, July 13th 1897.

Unfortunately, two years later in 1899 the school closed and the pupils were transferred to Great Haywood as funds could not be found to carry on as a voluntary school, and the managers did not wish to become a Board School.

Craven Vincent remained Rector of Tixall for 22 years, until 1906, when the Rev James Walton arrived at the Rectory in December.

Following a survey in January 1906, repairs to the Rectory had been completed at a total estimated cost of £58.[112]

The quarry tiles in the kitchen were again giving trouble with instructions to take up and reinstate about 3 sq yds by the Range, as well as :-

Scullery - Reinstate Norfolk Latch to door. reset oak curb to furnace and repair quarry top. Repair and point grate.

Boot House - Door and window

Fowl House - Door

Loft over Fowl House - Point up stone steps. Norfolk Latch.

Exterior:-

Outside WC Norfolk Latch

Yard Gate

Chimney Stacks

Roofs

Elevations:- .. cut off all ivy from verges and eaves.

Yard walls - reinstate capping to Yard door

Stable Buildings:-

Stables No.1 & 2 - Relay uneven floor - reinstate stall division
Rehang door into Coach House - Norfolk Latch

Coach House - reinstate fire grate, repair double doors

Saddle Room - reinstate fire grate

Paint outside ... but not front Entrance Gate or buildings with galvanized roofs beyond saddle room in yard.

Color the exterior walls of house and buildings 2 coats as previously done.

Minor repairs were also carried to the Church at the same time:-
Chancel to Church
Exterior - Remove all moss from tiles and reinstate any missing tiles.
Rake out and fill up with cement, open joints in stonework at level of
ground.

The Church heating had continued to be a source of concern
and on April 13th 1903, the Minutes recorded:-[111]
"It was found that in consequence of the Churchwardens having to
buy a new boiler for the Church Heating Apparatus there was a debit
balance of £4 - 7s - 3d.
In order to wipe off this debt it was proposed by the Rector and
seconded by Mr Hunt, that on Sunday week the 26th April there be
special collections at both services.

Further work was carried out in 1909 when the following
account was sent to the Churchwardens by Rudge & Griffith of
Stafford Foundry,[118] a copy of the second sheet is given on page 111:-

Sept 2nd	4	3 x 3 Steel Joists 9ft	£3 - - 24	10/-	£1 - 12 - 2
		Cutting ditto to length 4 cuts			
	1	24 x 17 Manhole Cover			
		& frame coated	£1 - 2 - 4	12/-	18 - 5
	9	W J Hooks for ditto		6	1
To Bricklayers a/c altering boiler House of Hot Water apparatus					
Sept 4th		100 red Bricks, Mortar			
		& Carting	19 - 6		
		Bricklayer & Laborer	£1 - 4 - 7		
Sept 11th		600 Red Bricks, Mortar,			
		Nails, 9 cwt Cement	£2 - 15		
		1 ton 15cwt Granite Chippings,			
		Fine Sand & Carting	£1 - 18 - 3		
		Bricklayer & Laborer 50 hrs	£3 - 1 - 5½		
Sept 25th		Cement, Plaster, Fine			
		Sand & Carting	19 - 2½		

(Cont. page 112)

TELEGRAMS: "RUDGE, STAFFORD." TELEPHONE Nº 56.

Stafford Foundry, Stafford, 31 Jany, 1909

The Churchwardens of Niall Church,

Dr to Rudge & Griffith

Engineers & Ironfounders,

MANUFACTURERS OF

Bridges, Girders, Fencing, Agricultural Implements, Stoves, Grates

& EVERY DESCRIPTION OF WROUGHT & CAST IRONWORK.

HOT WATER APPLIANCES FOR HEATING PUBLIC BUILDINGS, MANUFACTORIES, &c.

			s	d		£	s	d
	Forward		12	6½		2	14	7
⅓ x 25	Jornier & time 2½ hours		1	10½				
			12	2				
	To superintending do. 109.	1	4	3		13	6	8
	" Railway Expenses						2	
Jan 20	" examining & repg							
	Door of Heating							
	apparatus boiler							
	1 Wrought Surge Pin							3
	Fitters time 7½ hours					9	5	8
	Railway Expenses					1	4	
	By allowance				£	16	10	6
							7	3
						16	3	3

Bricklayer & Laborer 10hrs   12 - 3½
To window frame 6' 6" of 4½ x ½, Nails, Wire Netting, Staples,
      Timber for centre & cutting   10 - 3
      Joiners time 2½ hours   1 - 10½
                            £12 - 2 - 5
   To superintending 10%   1 - 4 -3   13 - 6 - 8
   Railway Expenses   2
Jan 20th   To examining repairing Door of Heating apparatus boiler
      1 W... F..... Pin, Fitters time 7½ hours   5 - 8
      Railway Expenses   1 - 4
                                 16 - 10 - 6
             By Allowance   7 - 3
                                 16 - 3 - 3

On March 11th 1908 a Confirmation was held at Tixall Church when the following local people were confirmed:-[119]

Geo Belcher
Geo Jas Millward
Thos Arthur Newman
Jas Allen Walker
Mrs Millward
Emily Frances Hollies
Lily Maud Heritage
Ada Belcher
Mrs Lizzie Clarke

No doubt this large number was due to the enthusiasm of a new Rector.

In 1910 the Rev. Harold Smith arrived, and in 1912 there was another large group of Tixall candidates for confirmation at Hixon Church on March 26th:-

William Gorbel
Peter Dodd
Richard Sargent
Alice Wetton
Lily Belcher
Bertha Hocknell
Ellen Clark
Annie Clark
Lucy Bamford

Probably with encouragement from the new Rector Tixall Church was voicing its opinion on Welsh Disestablishment at this time. The minutes of April 10th 1912,[111] record:-

"Copies of the following sent to the P.M., Home Secretary, Leader of the Opposition, and the Members for this division - proposed by Mr Nesbitt.

" The Parishioners of Tixall, in Easter Vestry assembled, strongly protest against the proposal to dismember the Church by cutting off from the Province of Canterbury the four Welsh Dioceses and to despoil it by confiscation to secular uses endowments consecrated to the service of God."

On March 18th 1909 the following Table of Fees was approved for Tixall Church, which gives some idea of the kind of services which could have been held:-

Matter or thing in respect of which a Fee is payable	Fee payable to Minister (incl. of Surplice Fees)	Fee payable to Clerk	Fee payable to Sexton or Gravedigger
Baptism. Fees are forbidden by Act 35 & 36 Vict 2.36	Nil	Nil	Nil
Marriage by Banns (incl. publication of Banns)	4s - 6d	2s - 0d	Nil

Matter or thing in respect of which a Fee is payable	Fee payable to Minister (incl. of Surplice Fees)	Fee payable to Clerk	Fee payable to Sexton or Gravedigger
Publication of Banns in a Church other than that in which the marriage is celebrated, and for Certifcate of such publication	2s - 0d	0s - 6d	Nil
Marriage by Licence	10s - 0d	5s - 0d	Nil
Churching of Women	A	Voluntary	Offering
Tolling Bell at time of Death	Nil	Nil	1s - 0d
Burial of Stillborn Infant under 5 years	Nil	Nil	1s - 6d
Burial of Infant under 5 years	2s - 6d	Nil	2s - 0d
Burial of Parishioner in ordinary grave 5ft in depth	3s - 6d	2s-0d	8s - 0d on north side of path 3s - 6d on the south side
Burial in new brick grave, single width	£2 - 2s - 0d	2s - 6d	6s 0d For grave 6ft in depth and 1/6 for every foot beyond that depth*
Burial in new brick grave, double width	£4 - 4s - 0d	5s - 0d	10s - 0d and 2/6 for every foot beyond that depth*

Matter or thing in respect of which a Fee is payable	Fee payable to Minister (incl. of Surplice Fees)	Fee payable to Clerk	Fee payable to Sexton or Gravedigger
Monumental Brass or Tablet in Church (not exceeding 10 superficial feet)**	£5 - 5s - 0d	Nil	Nil
For every additional superficial foot	10s - 0d	Nil	Nil
Brass plate attached to a Memorial Window (not exceeding one superficial foot)**	10s - 0d	Nil	Nil
Monument other than as above, or attachment in Church**	£10 - 10s 0d	Nil	Nil

* This fee does not include charges for Bricklayer or Mason
** These cannot be erected without a Faculty the fees for which are not included
NB. Double Fees for non Parishioners except for burial in Vaults or Brick Graves

In addition to the Fees mentioned in the forgoing Table, which are fixed by the Ecclesiastical Commissioners for England, the following fees fixed by Act of Parliament are payable to the Incumbent, viz:-

[See Act 6 & 7 W IV c86, sec.35]
Stamped Certificate of Baptism, Marriage or Burial   2s - 7d
Searching Register (for the first year)   1s - 0d
Searching Register (for every year after the first)   0s - 6d

[See Act 6 & 7 W IV c71 sec 64]
Inspection of Tyhthe Map and Instruments of Apportionment   2s - 6d
(If in the custody of the Incumbent)
Extract from Tither Apportionment (For every 72 words)   0s - 3d

In the 1920's the Sunday Services were as follows:-[120]

    8.00 Holy Communion
  11.00 Mattins (& Communion)
    3.00 Children's Service
    6.30 Evensong

In August 1920, the Rector the Rev.H.Smith was given a quote of around £60 by Robert Bridgeman & Sons of Lichfield, for Limewood figures with an Oak Cross and Pedestals for the rood.[121]

In November it was decided to lengthen the cross to raise the central figure so that additional attendant figures could be added later, and they would then be below the central figure.

A brass plate was to record:-

" The Rood in this Church is dedicated to the Memory of
    George Gill   North. Fusiliers
    Henry Victor Ellement   S.Staffs Reg.
    Edward Walker   N.Staffs.Reg.

The total estimated cost was £85.

The rood beam came from Ingestre probably free of charge. It was reduced from 10" to 8", and " a small rotten knot on the back side" cut out and repaired by Mr Bradbury of Haywood.

In June 1921 the Rector asked for a brass plate about 20 x 10 inches, surrounded by a plain double line border with two additional names:-

    William Harrison Notts & Derby
    Harry Towers   1st Border Reg.

It is interesting that at some time there was a change of plan, as the present plaque with the 5 names in the nave by the chancel arch, is of alabaster with a decorated border.

The dedication service on Sunday July 3rd 1921, was reported in the Staffordshire Advertiser.[122]

The Bishop of Lichfield performed the dedication ceremony, while the Rev.H.Smith, Rector of Tixall took the service.

. The hymns were: "O God Our Help in Ages Past", "When I surveyed the Wondrous Cross" and "Soldiers who art Christ's below".

The Bishop preached from the text:" But God forbid that I should glory save in the cross of our Lord Jesus Christ, by Whom the world is crucified unto me, and I unto the world." (Galations vi.14)

"The singing of "Ten thousand times ten thousand" and the Benediction by the Bishop, brought an appropriate and memorable service to a close."

The Churchwardens were F.J.Nesbitt and Samuel Dodd. They both served as Churchwarden for 30 years from 1905 until 1934, Mr Nesbitt as Rectors Warden and Mr Dodd as Parishioners Warden.

Frederick John Nesbitt lived at Tixall Lodge, with his wife Marion Eleanor from about 1902 until 1923, when they probably moved to Broc Hill, Milford.

Three of his children were baptised at Tixall:-
Joan on June 5th 1902 -father's occupation given as Gentleman
Humphrey John Stuart on June 30th 1906 -   "   Brewer
Noreen on November 7th 1911 -   "   "

The brewer connection may explain why the public house on Churchill Way off the Wolverhampton Road , is called the Nesbitt Arms.

In 1920 there were two breweries listed in Stafford:- J.Dawson in Sandon Road and Eley's Stafford Brewery Ltd. on the Green.[123]

In 1952 a matching limestone plaque with the Nesbitt shield was put up to mark the completion of the rood.

The plaque reads:-
" THE FIGURES OF OUR LADY AND S.JOHN WERE ADDED TO THE ROOD IN THIS CHURCH TO THE GLORY OF GOD AND IN LOVING MEMORY OF FREDERICK JOHN NESBITT, HIS WIFE

MARION ELEANOR, AND THEIR SON HUMPHREY JOHN
STUART NESBITT.   1952

Frederick had died in 1935 aged 75, Marion in 1938 aged 67, and their son Humphrey in 1942 aged 36, at Queen Elizabeth's Hospital, Birmingham.

The Nesbitt shield also occurs at the Nesbitt Arms Public House, and are described as :-
> Agent on a chevron
> Gulles between 3 boars heads
> coupled Sable
> a Scottish thistle leaved proper.[124]

It is interesting that the thistle is only present on the shield at Tixall.

When the Archdeacon of Stafford visited the Church on May 5th 1925, he reported:-
> "I visited this Church, accompanied by the Rural Dean.
> The Church is well kept and the fabric in good order.
> The insurance on the fabric is inadequate and to be increased by at least £1,650.
> A plan to be made of the grave-yard.
> The ivy on the Church to be well cut in and not allowed to grow higher than 3 or 4 ft off the roof."

This ivy is shown in a postcard of 1910 reaching almost to the church bell. (Page 119)

The Church was obviously thriving in the 1920s as substantial numbers of candidates were presented for confirmation in 1924, 1925 and 1927.[120]

On May 12 1924 at St Chad's, Stafford the following were confirmed from Tixall:-

Males:- C.Betts
    J.W.Walters
    J.D.Ellwood
    W.Foster
    J.C.Foster
    A.J.Belcher

Females:- L.M.Wareham
     E.V.Holmes
     A.E.Ellwood
     M.Silvester
     E.M.Ellwood

On March 13th,1925 the following were confirmed at Colwich:-

Males:- G.Silvester

Females:- K.Hyndman
     M.Hyndman
     E.Jackson
     E.Tamms
     H.Seer
     B.Rowson
     M.Clements
     E.Mort

And on November 22nd, 1927, the following were confirmed at

Walton:-   Jane Brooks
                            Constance Mayhew
                            Eva Stevens
                            Evelyn Ellwood
                            Gertrude Johnson
                            Constance Collier

Harold Smith left after 18 years in 1928, and there followed a four year interregnum until the parish was combined with Ingestre in 1933, under the Hon.Sydney George William Maitland who lived at Ingestrey Rectory.

During the interregnum Tixall was served by Henry H.Jevons, Vicar of St Chads; J.W.Barnsley, Ass.Curate at St Pauls; W.Barnes Hunter, Retired Vicar of Croxton (who lived at Tixall Villa); Alfred Ebrey, late Vicar of Childs Ercall; and S.G.W.Maitland, Rector of Ingestre.

Consequently, Tixall Rectory was let to Marshall Arthur B.Landers from 1934 until 1938, when Clifford William Dugmore became Rector of the two parishes.

On April 18th, 1933, the first Tixall vestry and annual meeting under the new Rector showed considerable activity:-[111]

There were 60 on the Electoral Roll, and 15 boys and 40 girls in the Sunday School.

The Good Friday alms (4/7) were allocated to the Lental Boxes Fund. The Rector suggested that the Whit Sunday Collection should go to the Church Missionary overseas.

The Rector was to start a joint Parish Magazine with Ingestre.

The question of increasing the organ blowers wages was discussed in view of the additional work involved during choir practice. Mr Dodd was instructed to interview Mr Bamford about terms, 30/- was suggested instead of £1.

Mr Wilton had £2 - 10s in hand from last years choir outing fund, and it was decided to pay the following 10/- each:- Messrs. Foster, Belcher, Collier, Bamford and Morris.

The large chalice in the secretaries charge to be valued and kept in Barclays Bank.

Miss Hall was thanked for attending to the altar flowers.

The following meeting reported that the Church Plate had been valued as follows:-

Large Chalice...................£85 to be kept at Bank and not insured

Other Chalice.................£30

Paten...........................£75 both to be insured all risks

This must have been the original large paten which is now kept at Lichfield Heritage Centre with the large chalice.

In 1936 an estimate of £42 was obtained to install electric lighting in the Church, including the service line.

It was agreed that this expenditure could not be met from Church Funds, but a special fund was opened with guarantees of £27 given at the meeting.

In August 1937 a joint meeting was held with Ingestre to discuss the appointment of a new incumbent.

It was noted that they could make formal representations for the Churchwardens to meet the patron; do nothing; or make a written representation to the patron setting out the needs, circumstances and traditions of the Parishes, but without indicating in any manner the appointment of a particular individual.[111]

As the Earl of Shrewsbury was well aware of the present situation it was agreed by 5 votes for and 5 against to do nothing.

The Rector than proposed an informal meeting with Lord Shrewsbury.

On July 21st 1938 the Rev. Clifford Dugmore was given a very hearty welcome to the Church Council, and at the following meeting in November, Mr H.Collier was thanked for having had the electric light put in the Church Porch.

It was also agreed to use the old school building as a Parish Hall.

The following year, 1939, the annual meeting again showed significant activity:-

Mrs Hill was thanked for her continuing work in connection with the vestments and altar flowers.

Thanks were also expressed to Lord Shrewsbury for the loan of his Rotoscythe which had enabled them to clear the Churchyard, and to Mrs Mynors for collecting money for rose trees and other improvements to the Churchyard.

There were a good number of candidates for confirmation, and it was hoped that the numbers attending Holy Communion would continue to increase.

"Meetings such as this were necessary, but it was even more necessary to remember the spiritual work on which we were engaged as members of the family of Christ."

It is interesting that there were no meetings of the Church Council between May 1939 and March 1940, because of the blackout restrictions.

Problems were also being experienced in getting the Boiler stoked often enough to heat the Church satisfactorily on Sunday, because Mr Spink. the sexton and verger, lived at Ingestre.

In May 1940, it was agreed to install an electric blower for the organ, as Peter Spink had indicated his desire to terminate his employment, and there was no suitable replacement.

In 1941 the Rector, the Rev.Dugmore agreed to act as stoker "during the present emergency", presumably because Mr Spink was resigning as Verger and Sexton.

It was agreed that the Churchyard should be scythed twice a year and that mowing should be continued for the duration of the war.

It was reported that the heating apparatus was in very bad condition, but the Rector would have to write to the Ministry of Supply for a certificate for the use of the necessary steel for a new electrical system.

It was thought unlikely that this would be granted.

The boiler was therefore replaced in 1942 at a cost of £39 - 19s - 4 d which was covered by a house to house collection of £42 - 14s 6d.

The Rector noted that the letting of the Parish Room in a small place like Tixall, could never meet the overhead charges, and that the room was a Church Room used for Church purposes as well as entertainment.

Mrs Holmes was appointed as local representative for the Womens Emergency Land Corps.

In 1943 the Rev.Fisher became Rector and in July the Church Council meeting noted:-

Vestments to be worn in Church, to be left to the Rector to wear what he liked.

It is interesting that it usually takes some years for things to actually happen at Tixall, hence in April, 1946, new hangings on the pattern of the English Altar were to be investigated.

In April the following year it was noted that the Altar frontals and Sanctuary hangings were sadly in need of renewal and a sub-committee was set up with Mrs Fisher (the Rector's wife) Mrs Phillimore, Mrs Collier, and Mrs Hillsdon.

By September estimates had been obtained, and in January 1948, the green altar frontal had arrived.

The Rector ordered a new pulpit fall and bookmarker to correspond with it.

A purple altar frontal was being made, and the present pulpit fall and bookmarker would correspond with that.

This led to extensive alterations around the altar. A faculty dated 10th March authorises:-[125]

" New 6ft high Riddel Posts, joined by a carved oak mold from which a Dossal is hung, and candlesticks, octagonal with circular caps, for a total cost of £16 -10s.

Blue Fairford brocade and curtains:-- £38 - 5s

Design by Messrs James & Willis Ltd.

and removal of common deal reredos (with applique paper monograms) which has been hidden by curtains many years.

and removal of a flight of shelves forming a re-table at the back of the Altar table.

shelves to be used as book shelf as and when required.

Reredos is valueless except that approx. date of Church is believed to be 13th Century rebuilt 1849"

In April 1950 it was reported that the Ridell Posts and Curtains had been dedicated by the Archdeacon.

Despite all this activity, attendance at Church was poor. In April 1946:

Mr Collier had expressed concern at the absence from Church of Wage Earning Men in the Parish, and hoped that efforts to revive their interest in, and attendance at Church, might be made.

Mr Collier expressed his concern that so many parishioners had ceased to attend Church, the following year, and methods to deal with this were discussed.

In February 1948 the Rector noted that:-

The congregation at Matins remained static, though the parishioners in general seemed indifferent to the duty of regular public worship, attendance at Holy Communion, especially at early service leaves much to be desired, while at Evensong is improving chiefly through the attendance of some young people.

Gratitude was expressed to the organist and choir.

The Sunday School continues to grow.

Mothers Union is a bright spot, the meetings being much enjoyed by the members, and not less by the children who are encouraged to attend with them, and for whom special provision is made.

Part of the plan for beautifying the altar has been carried out.

Organ cleaned and repaired.

Gifts of a new Hymn Board and a Weeping Standard Rose for the Churchyard.

Parish Room being increasingly used for Tixall Social Club & WI. Electrical heating installed at the expense of Messrs Rowland, Collier and Bostock, and is much appreciated.

Finally the Rector stated that while financially the Church and Parish was in a sound condition, too much importance cannot be stressed on the spiritual side of the Church's work and the need for the Council to further this quoting the Enabling Act " that the primary duty of the Church Council is in every Parish to co-operate with the incumbent in the initiation, conduct and development of Church work, within and outside the parish."

There is not sufficient space or time to recount all the details of the more recent history of Tixall Church.

Suffice to say that following the retirement of the Rev. Arthur Poole in 1980, attempts were made to unite the Churches of Tixall and Ingestre with either Haywood or Berkswich, and eventually a joint benefice with St John's, Littleworth was formed under the Rev. E.G.H. Townshend.

This would appear to be a fitting union as the site of the Church and School at Littleworth, were donated by the Earl of Shrewsbury, alongwith stone from Tixall Hall, demolished in 1926. The Tixall stone being used to build the vestry and chancel at St John's, Littleworth.

The small population at Tixall continues the struggle to maintain the fabric of their Church as a visible sign of the health of the Christian Community in Tixall.

APPENDIX

DATE	CHURCHWARDENS	
1682	Dick Wall (His mark)	
1685	Joshuah Preston	Anthony Hawthorn
1693	Joshuah Weston ?	Anthony Horthan (His mark)
1698	Joshua Preston	John Sawyer
1702	Thomas Kent	George Lander
1705	John Robins	George Lander
1708	William Malpas	
1714	Joshua Preston (His mark)	Tom Kinson
1718	Joshua Preston (His mark)	John Sawyer
1722	Richard Tomkinson	Edward Proston ?
1732		Edward Proston
1735	Wm Baily	
1738		Edward Proston
1741	Wm Baily	
1747	Wm Bailey ?	
1758	Wm Clegg	
1762	Wm Clegg	
1773	John Cliff	
1776	John Cliff	
1782	John Cliff	
1786	John Cliff	
1791	John Clegg	
1809	Preston Moore Cliff	
1845	John Scott ?	
1849-1855	James Tyrer	

	RECTORS WARDEN	PARISHIONERS WARDEN
1856-1860	James Tyrer	James Warner
1861-1864	Walter Holden Steward	James Warner
1865-1866	Joseph Ford	James Warner
1867-1869	Thomas Bottley	James Warner
1870-1871	Edward Mayne	James Warner
1872	Edward Mayne	
1873-1874	William Power	

	RECTORS WARDEN	PARISHIONERS WARDEN
1875-1876	William Power	W.C.T.Mynors
1877-1878	William Power	G.A.Hodgson
1879	Henry Dodd	G.A.Hodgson
1880-1881	Joseph Ford	G.A.Hodgson
1882	Thomas H.Dodd	Joseph Ford
1883-1884	Henry Dodd	Earl of Shrewsbury
1885-1897	Henry Dodd	Lord Shrewsbury
1899-1904	George Stretton	Lord Shrewsbury
1905-1928	F.J.Nesbitt	Samuel Dodd
1933-1934	F.J.Nesbitt	Samuel Dodd
1935-1939	R.Cave Rogers	G.Parrott
1940-1945	W.H.Rowland	G.Parrott
1940	*Humphrey Nesbitt*	*Deputy Churchwarden*
1941-1944	*J.Brooks*	*Deputy Churchwarden*
1946-1947	W.H.Rowland	Phillimore
1948	W.H.Rowland	J.Fairbanks
1949-1953	G.Parrott	J.Fairbanks
1954-1961	Kenneth Stott	J.Fairbanks
1954	*G.Parrott*	*Deputy Churchwarden*
1961-1964	E.Phillips	J.Fairbanks
1964-1966	E.Phillips	M.Denham
1967	E.Phillips	Mr Giles
1968	E.Phillips	R.Collier ?

NO RECTORS OR PARISHIONERS WARDENS FROM 1968

1969-1970	R.Collier	
1971	R.Collier	G.Bostock
1972-1978	No Vestry or PCC Meetings Minuted	
1979-1983	P.H.Collier	G.Bostock
1984	M.Snape	G.Bostock
1985-1986	M.Snape	M.Sindrey
1987-1988	Robert Collier	M.Sindrey
1989	Robert Collier	P.H.Collier
1990-1991	Robert Collier	Phyllis Hill
1992-1993	M.Snape	Anne Andrews
1994-1995	M.Snape	Mary Kershaw

REFERENCES

Lichfield Joint Record Office   (LJRO)
Staffordshire Record Office   (SRO)
William Salt Library   (WSL)

1. Greenslade, M.W. and Stuart,D.G.
                A History of Staffordshire   1984 Phillimore & Co.Ltd.
2. Morris, John (Ed.)Domesday Book   24. Staffordshire
                                1976 Phillimore & Co.Ltd.
3. Clifford, Thomas and Clifford, Arthur
        A Topographical and Historical description of the Parish of
                Tixall in the County of Stafford   1817 Paris
4. Lambert, Lionel
        Ingestre and Tixall: Two Chapelries of the Royal Free Chapel
        or College of Stafford   1940 R.W.Hourd & Son, Stafford
5. Pitt, William   A Topographical History of Staffordshire
                                1817 Newcastle under Lyme
6. Sant, Desmond B. The Ancient Parish of Berkswich Part 1.1988
7. Collections for a History of Staffordshire 1883 vol.iv p112
8. Collections for a History of Staffordshire 1916 p199
9. Collections for a History of Staffordshire 1909 vol.xii ns p191
10. Collections for a History of Staffordshire 1909 vol.xii ns p171
11. Collections for a History of Staffordshire 1885 vol.vi pt1 p176
12. Collections for a History of Staffordshire 1884 vol.v pt1 p165
13. Collections for a History of Staffordshire 1905 vol.viii ns pxiii
14. Collections for a History of Staffordshire 1913 vol ns p308
15. Collections for a History of Staffordshire 1891 vol.xii p212
16. Collections for a History of Staffordshire 1890 vol.xi p244
17. Collections for a History of Staffordshire 1890 vol.xi p237
18. Collections for a History of Staffordshire 1892 vol.xiii p232
19. Collections for a History of Staffordshire 1892 vol.xiii p230
20. Collections for a History of Staffordshire 1900 vol.iii ns p33/34
21. Collections for a History of Staffordshire 1911 p103

22. Collections for a History of Staffordshire 1886 vol.vii pt1 p118
23. Collections for a History of Staffordshire 1911 p98
24. Collections for a History of Staffordshire 1903 vol.vi ns pt1 p130
25. Collections for a History of Staffordshire 1886 vol.vii p200
26. Collections for a History of Staffordshire 1889 vol.x pt1 p90
27. Collections for a History of Staffordshire 1893 vol.xiv p51
28. Collections for a History of Staffordshire 1921 p24
29. Collections for a History of Staffordshire 1909 p191
30. Betley, J.H. Church and Parish. A guide for Local Historians
1987 Batsford
31. Collections for a History of Staffordshire 1903 p187
32. Collections for a History of Staffordshire 1915 p289
33. Collections for a History of Staffordshire 1917 p329
34. Collections for a History of Staffordshire 1979 4th series vol.ix
p15/16
35. Collections for a History of Staffordshire 1932 p157
36. Tixall Letters I   Letter XVI   London 1815
37. Tixall Letters I   Letter XVII   London 1815
38. Collections for a History of Staffordshire 1903 vol.vi ns pt2 p331
39. Collections for a History of Staffordshire 1921 vol. p68
40. Probate Records Feb 26th 1617/18 1126.19 (LJRO)
41. Collections for a History of Staffordshire 1909 p195
42. Glebe Terrier 1676 B/V/6 (LJRO)
43. Glebe Terrier 1682 B/V/6 (LJRO)
44. Glebe Terrier 1735 B/V/6 (LJRO)
45. Calvert, Charles "History of and guide to Stafford"   1886
46. Cherry, J.L. and Cherry, Karl   "Historical Studies relating
chiefly to Staffordshire" p72 J.C.Mort Ltd. Stafford M.C.M.VII
47. Pbox T/1 Stephen Dugdale (Source Unidentified) published 1794
48. Haslam, Charlotte Ingestre Pavilion History
Landmark Trust 1991
49. Probate Records April 4th 1698 732.19 (LJRO)
50. Glebe Terrier 1722 B/V/6 (LJRO)
51. Glebe Terrier 1732 B/V/6 (LJRO)

52. Collections for a History of Staffordshire 1982 4th series vol.xi
                                                                    p77
53. Knight, Randle   Staffordshire History 1991 <u>13</u> p6
54. Probate Record May 20th 1742 303.16 (LJRO)
55. Tixall Presentation 20th May 1742 B/A/3 (LJRO)
56. Tixall Presentation 3rd August 1742 B/A/3 (LJRO)
57. Probate Record Dec 27th 1760 333.21 (LJRO)
58. Bibliotheca Staffordiensis compiled by Rupert Simms
                                                    Lichfield 1894
59. Glebe Terrier 1776 B/V/6 (LJRO)
60. Glebe Terrier 1786 B/V/6 (LJRO)
61. Pbox T/1 Tixall (WSL) Correspondence between the Rector
                           & RC Chaplain of Sir Clifford Constable 1833
62. Pbox T/1 Tixall (WSL)
          Catalogue of the Library of the Rev.W.Corne, Rector 1883
63. 2672 XI 34 (WSL)
64. Trent Valley Parochial Magazine 1871
                                 ANNALS OF TIXALL No.10 p27
65. Staffordshire Advertiser June 2nd 1849 p4
66. Guide & History of Ancient Haywood, Nr Stafford.
    Compiled & illustrated by Stafforda Cornish Brothers Ltd.
                                       Birmingham 1924
67. 2673 XI 23 (WSL)
68. Lichfield Diocesan Registry
69. CB/TIXALL/4 (WSL)
70. Collections for a History of Staffordshire 1950 p120
71. Collections for a History of Staffordshire 1960 4th series vol.iii
                                                                   p133
72. Oxford Dictionary of French Literature
73. Probate Record <u>6</u> 1751 - 1775 499.20 (LJRO)
74. Tixall Presentation 29th March 1823 B/A/3 (LJRO)
75. Nomination of Curates Tixall July 1826 B/A/11A (LJRO)
76. Collections for a History of Staffordshire 1980 4th series vol.10
                                                                    p69

77. Staffordshire Advertiser December 3rd 1864 p5
78. Reed, Brian "Crewe Locomotive Works and its Men"
David & Charles 1982
79. The Railway Magazine January to June 1901 Vol.VIII p454
80. D3380/8/3 (SRO)
81. Clifford, Arthur "Tixall Poetry" p342
Longman, Hurst, Rees, Orme & Brown London
and John Ballantyne & Co. Edinburgh 1813
82. Staffordshire Catholic History 1966-7 vol.8 p19
83. Collections for a History of Staffordshire 1960 4th series vol.iii
p143
84. The Landmark Trust - Tixall Gatehouse
85. Staffordshire Advertiser October 28th 1837 p1
86. 2674 XI 24 (WSL)
87. 2675 XI 25 (WSL)
88. Staffordshire Catholic History 1974 vol.14 p582
89. Staffordshire Catholic History 1961 vol.1 p37
90. Pevsner, Nikolaus "The Buildings of England: Staffordshire."
Penguin Books 1974

91. Bishops Register Book 1847 - 1853 p164 (Lichfield Diocese)
92. Staffordshire Advertiser June 5th 1852 p4
93. D3380/4/12 (SRO)
94. D3380/8/4 (SRO)
95. D240/E(I)/3/11(SRO) Stone Quarry Ledger (Salt Quarries)
1846-1851
96. White "History, Gazetteer and Directory of Staffordshire"
Sheffield 1851
97. Greenslade,M.W. & Stuart,D.G. "A History of Staffordshire"
Phillimore & Co.Ltd. 1984
98. D3380/4/7 (SRO)
99. Staffordshire Advertiser May 29th 1852 p4
100. Trent Valley Parochial Magazine July 1871 p27.
101. Staffordshire Advertiser June 26th 1875

102. D240/D/78 (SRO)
103. D5326/1 (SRO)
104. Victoria County History vol.6 p249
105. Staffordshire Advertiser May 12th 1866 p7
106. Staffordshire Advertiser May 5th 1866 p6
107. Joan Exton "St Thomas' Church, Castletown, Stafford"
    The British Publishing Co. Gloucester 1972   S/5/1/2/top (WSL)
108. Anslow, Joan and Randall, Theo
"Around Stafford in Old Photographs" Alan Sutton Publishing 1991
109. Lichfield Diocese Registry Office
110. Undated Newspaper Cutting in St Chads Scrapbook -
               Storeroom/Parish Histories/Stafford/St Chads (WSL)
111. Tixall Parochial Church Council Minutes, Volume 1 (SRO)
112. B/A/13i (LJRO)
113. D3380/7/2 (SRO)
114. D240/D/25 (SRO)
115. D3380/7/6.6 (SRO)
116. D3380/7/6.87 (SRO)
117. D3380/7/6.203/4 (SRO)
118. D3380/3/4 (SRO)
119. D3380/2/1 (SRO)
120. D3380/2/2 (SRO)
121. D3380/4/2 (SRO)
122. Staffordshire Advertiser July 9th 1921 p10
123. Stafford Directory 1920 Halden & Haywood's Ltd (WSL)
124. N.Staffs Field Club Transactions 1992-93 p38
125. D3380/4/4 (SRO)